BUSY PARENTS:
LEAD YOUR CHILDREN TO SUCCESS

GABRIEL SILVA

Copyright © 2014 by Gabriel Silva
All rights reserved. This book or any portion thereof
may not be reproduced or used in any manner whatsoever
without the express written permission of the publisher
except for the use of brief quotations in a book review.

First Printing 2014
ISBN 978-0-9921087-0-0
Academic Leaders Education Co.
#51524 – 911 Park Royal South
West Vancouver, BC, V7T 1A1, Canada
www.acleaders.com

This book is dedicated to my parents for being extremely supportive throughout my school years (and beyond), to Olga K. for the past five and a half (great) years, to all parents of students I have worked with throughout the past twelve years, and finally to all ambitious students seeking academic success.

TABLE OF CONTENTS

Introduction 11

Chapter 1: Tutoring 19

    What If I Am Not Sold on Tutoring? 20

    So what's the Ideal Definition of Tutoring? 23

    The Tutor's Personality and Demeanor 24

    Building Rapport during Tutoring Sessions—A Waste of Time? 26

    Looking for a Good Match between Student and Tutor 29

    The "Shotgun Approach" 30

    Loyalty in Tutoring—A Closer Look (And How to Move On) 32

    Finding a Good Tutor—Local Agencies and Tutoring Businesses 34

    What about Free Tutoring? 37

    Finding a Good Independent Tutor 39

    What Should You Be Flexible about When Hiring a Tutor? 41

    The Tutor's Hourly Rate—What It Can Tell You 43

    Should I Hire a "Cheap" Tutor If I Have a Tight Budget? 45

    A Note on the Tutor's Gender, Age and Background 47

    So what should one look for in a tutor? 48

    What to Ask from an Independent Tutor 49

    Interviewing a Tutor 49

    Online Tutors—Are They a Good Choice? 51

    What about Group Tutoring? Is It a Good Idea? 51

    Finding a Good Tutor on a Budget 53

Chapter 2: The Academic Team 57

    Introducing the Main Roles within an Academic Team 60

        The Subject Expert 61

        The Motivator 61

        The Planner 62

    The Discipline Coach 63

Forming the Team with All Different Roles 64

Getting the Student On Board with Getting Help 65

Important Note: The Title of a Professional & Student Reluctance 71

Taking a Closer Look at the Four Main Roles 73

    The Role of the Subject Expert 73

    The Role of the Motivator 76

    The Role of the Planner 86

    The Role of the Discipline Coach 88

Leading Students versus "Babying" Them 93

Developing the Perfect Academic Team: "the System" 94

    Recognizing Needs 94

    Setting a Framework 97

    Evaluating Professionals 98

    Reaching Out 99

    Managing 101

Paying for the Academic Team on a Budget 103

How Much Input Should the Student Have Regarding the Team? 104

Communicating with the Team 106

    Communicating Expectations 106

    Requesting Utmost Honesty 107

    Frequency of Communication & Using Mini-Reports 108

    Asking for Updates in Front of the Student 112

The Team's Relationship with the School Staff 113

Chapter 3: Common Issues—Strategies and Tips 115

The Student Hits a Plateau—Complacency Sets In 116

How to Avoid Complacency Altogether 119

When & How to "Step In" 122

Dealing with an Academic Crisis 125

    When the Student's Results Are Lower than Expected 125

    What If the Professional from the Academic Team Is to Blame? .. 126

    What If the Student Is to Blame? 128

  Student-Teacher Dynamic 129

    What If the Student Has a Bad Relationship with the Teacher? 129

  Overdependence on the Academic Team 132

    How to Avoid the Pitfalls Thereof 132

Chapter 4: Students—Approaching Their Uniqueness 135

  What (Academic) Level is the Student Currently At? 136

    Level "A" Students 137

    Level "B" Students 138

    Level "C" Students 141

  Students with Learning Disabilities 143

  Students with Very Busy Schedules 144

    Balancing Sports and Academics 144

    Successfully Balancing Academics with Other Activities 149

Chapter 5: Student Psychology—Strategies and Considerations 151

  General Strategy—Getting Students to Stick to Commitments 152

  Getting Students to Stop Doubting Their Abilities 154

  Selling and Embracing Persistence 158

  Debunking the "Hollywood" View of Success Once and for All 161

  Handling Competition in a Healthy Way 162

  Dealing with Boredom and Lack of Patience in Students 163

Chapter 6: Case Studies 167

  Melanie (Busy Student & Academic Team on a Budget) 168

  Duncan (Independent Student with a Low B Average) 172

  Christopher (From Barely Passing to Straight As) 178

INTRODUCTION

Introduction

For me, few things are as noble as the deeply genuine desire of parents to help their children in any way they can. It's beautiful and sincere, and once this desire comes to fruition, it simply makes the world a better place, since it leads children to thrive, enabling them to have a positive effect in society. During my twelve years in the tutoring industry (five years as an independent tutor and another seven running a renowned tutoring business in Vancouver, British Columbia), I have often heard parents say, "I want to help my child do better in school, but I just have no idea how to go about it." It became clear to me that parents, especially busy ones, would greatly benefit from clear and concise, time-tested guidance on how to help their children get motivated, gain hope, become more confident, set their sights higher, and do better in school. All of what I present in this book comes from over a decade of hands-on experience helping students reach their potential, while giving parents the tools to do the same.

Additionally, I have witnessed what has and hasn't worked for most parents and their children on their quest for academic success. These elements helped me shape the straightforward suggestions, thoughts, and strategies I present in this book. With this new arsenal of tools, parents will have more power to help students get inspired to relentlessly pursue their dreams with unforeseen confidence and motivation.

Most of the parents of students I worked with had already taken the most common steps in response to academic underachievement: nagging their children to study hard, going to parent–teacher conferences, hiring tutors and, in the end, letting go and hoping for the best. Many parents would tell me they felt hopeless; there just wasn't much else they could do when their children's grades weren't as high as expected. Unfortunately, their investment often did not translate into positive results. It was also unfortunate to hear about all the things they did in an attempt to help that didn't work out at all—and turned out to be a complete waste of time and (very often, lots of) money.

It was always with a certain degree of sadness that I would witness the parents' frustration. I would see these great students, who often had great potential, underperforming for various reasons, while the poor parents were trying their best to help without much result. This would make me sad because I was so inspired by their commitment to the well-being of their children, whom I strongly believed deserved to get motivated and become hopeful again.

Fortunately, all it usually takes for students to improve their grades is the right framework combined with a bit of a push. Very often, I worked with students who were able to improve significantly in a near-miraculous fashion. In many of these cases, all they needed was a combination of strategies and key elements, such as building rapport with a helpful professional or sharing their commitments for improvement with friends, which gave their confidence and motivation levels a bit of a boost so they could take flight. The ideas discussed in this book give parents various avenues to explore for making these key elements fall into place for their children.

A note for parents: Although you are welcome to skip the sections in which you might already have a lot of knowledge, I still strongly recommend that you go over all of them at one point or another. Moreover, I would like to ask you to seriously think about how to implement the information in this book as you take it in, especially when an idea might seem applicable and interesting. Viewing these ideas through the lens of practical action for your situation will enable you to put the suggestions to good use.

Chapter 1 takes a look at a very common engagement used by today's students in order to improve their grades and succeed at school—private tutoring. My primary goal in discussing tutoring (and exploring it in detail) is to analyze what aspects of

Introduction

this practice greatly contribute to students' progress. Another goal is to maximize tutoring's positive effects for families that are either currently using a tutor or are considering hiring one. Whether or not you are sold on the idea of getting a tutor, I highly suggest you read this chapter in detail.

Chapter 2 introduces the idea of an academic team and looks at the different roles that professionals can play in supporting a student. This crucial idea can have a compounding impact on a student's academic career. Chapter 3 further explores the student's mindset and offers time-tested tips and strategies that parents can use to support their children's quest for success.

Chapters 4 and 5 describe different situations that individual students might present and outline how to deal with them. In particular, Chapter 5 addresses the importance of respecting a student's psychology—something that is overlooked far too often—for these methods to work. By this I mean considering each student's behaviour, way of thinking, and mindset to craft a strategy that will effectively help that child succeed. Often, this simply comes down to honouring how unique each student is, and getting professionals to connect with him or her, building rapport on an individual basis. Once that is accomplished, the student opens up and becomes much more receptive to suggestions and tips.

Finally, Chapter 6 presents three case studies of students at different levels and in different situations in order to illustrate some of the ideas discussed in this book, which will help parents develop a clearer idea of how to apply some of the given strategies to their specific situations.

Failing to take a student's psychology into consideration can be very costly for everyone involved. Imagine, for instance, that a parent hires a tutor for a defiant student who isn't really on board with the process. The parent may gain some peace of mind from trying to help, but the whole venture will probably be completely fruitless unless the student actually starts appreciating the parent's efforts. The unfortunate thing is that situations like this one happen far more often than they should. The fortunate thing is that this book provides straightforward solutions for busy parents who actually want to overcome this type of issue and make a significant, positive impact on their children's academic life. However, this will be possible only if parents actually take a step back and get some clear insight into how to go about this process effectively, and help their child become fully committed to getting help.

Introduction

I strongly believe that the ideas presented in this book will significantly help busy parents in their quest to support their children in reaching their dreams. Of course, not all strategies will be effective for every student, so it is paramount that you test different ideas in order to find what works best for each individual student and each situation. With the right elements in place, you will very soon witness your student becoming more motivated, confident, and driven to succeed. At the very least, I am certain you will find great inspiration and practical ideas on how to promote your child's success.

CHAPTER 1: TUTORING

Chapter 1: Tutoring

Most of you are certainly quite familiar with the idea of tutoring. Even if you are, and even if you consider yourself an expert in hiring and managing tutors, I would still highly recommend that you carefully go over this section. Why is that? Because essentially, every tutor is different and every tutoring relationship develops differently. So it's great to take a step back and take a look at the ideal tutor and what the ideal tutoring relationship should look like. That way, parents can become more empowered in understanding what they should and can expect from a great tutor. Additionally, when (and if) necessary, parents can take steps to improve the tutoring arrangement with current professionals and, as a result, watch their children obtain more benefits from the extra support.

What If I Am Not Sold on Tutoring?

What if you aren't sold on the idea of getting a tutor for your children? Then I still highly recommend you go over this section since it can provide a good perspective on what could be achieved, what the ideal engagement should be like, and why so many people hire tutors nowadays. As I will point out at different points in this book, competition in the academic world has never been

Chapter 1: Tutoring

more intense. And guess what—most students nowadays do have tutors. Often I have heard parents say, "In my son's school, almost nobody has a tutor." Even in that case, remember that your children will be competing with many students from different schools around the country (and actually around the world) when they apply for a college and later when they are actually in college, and chances are that many of these students actually got extra support in the form of tutoring.

Something funny I have also heard plenty of times from parents is, "I know a guy who made it into this great school, and he said he actually never got any tutoring at all." That might be true, but it doesn't say much. Why not? First, it may just be that this person was lucky enough to have completely uncommon and quite fantastic work habits from the age of five. Or it could be that he has a photographic memory and lucked out on his standardized tests. It could be a combination of any or all of these factors. We don't know! Also, it could be that he lied and that he did get thousands of hours of tutoring. Even if he indeed got no tutoring, chances are he would have done even better in school if he had actually had tutors.

Apparently, not too long ago, tutoring used to be a bit of a secret thing. Nobody would say they received tutoring. Everyone was afraid they would be judged and that people would think their children weren't smart if they hired tutors. But nowadays, tutoring is a multi-billion dollar industry, which leads us to think that, well, more than just a handful of people are being tutored. That alone should be evidence enough that it works. After all, if it didn't, why would people continue to collectively waste billions of dollars on an ongoing basis?

Of course, the positive effects of tutoring are hard to measure, and they can certainly range from small to huge. From experience, I have often seen dramatic increases in students' grades after they started a regular tutoring program with a good tutor that they connected with. You could think I am biased; after all, I have been in the tutoring industry for over a decade, so of course I would speak in favour of it. But you can be sure that the reason I have been in it for this long is that I truly believe in it. And the reason I truly believe in it is that I have seen it work again and again.

I hope I managed to make you think about considering tutoring for your child, in case you were against tutoring before reading this book. If not, I would still encourage you to keep reading this chapter since many of the suggestions will likely be very beneficial when used in similar relationships and many of the motivational strategies presented could actually be employed by anyone.

So what's the Ideal Definition of Tutoring?

I would like to define tutoring as it should be, as opposed to what it usually or often is. Tutoring should be the dynamic process in which an engaging instructor (or academic mentor/coach) provides active support to a student in a specific academic subject, while inspiring the pupil to achieve his or her highest potential.

I realize this is a wordy definition, but it's what the ideal tutor should do. If you are getting a tutor to help your child, the chosen professional may as well be as close to this ideal as possible.

I would like to make a few observations here. The first one would be to stress the difference between tutoring and homework help, which could be defined simply as anyone helping students complete their homework. Of course, a tutor can assist a student with his or her homework, but tutoring should extend well beyond that. Why is that? Because there is minimal value in homework help. If a "tutor" is just basically doing a student's homework without properly engaging him or her, then the pupil is actually learning close to nothing while getting away with not doing the work they are supposed to be doing.

It takes skill to engage students and to give them the proper tools to step up and succeed, and unfortunately, not all tutors have that. Additionally, many lazy tutors will prefer to just do the student's homework and try to get away with it, later justifying the student's poor performance in exams by blaming the student in some way.

The Tutor's Personality and Demeanor

It is important for the tutor to have a good personality. Optimally, he or she should be a likeable individual to whom the student can relate. The professional doesn't necessarily have to be super charismatic but should hopefully be someone easy to get along with.

Now here is a key idea that I may bring up a few more times: <u>The student must enjoy working with the tutor in order for the effects of tutoring to be maximized.</u> If the student simply doesn't enjoy working with a particular tutor, it's often a worthless effort, and sometimes it could turn out to be a complete waste of everyone's time and your money.

Chapter 1: Tutoring

Additionally, it is important for the professional to have the sensibility to understand the limits of the students (and by the way, the same applies to parents). Often, when a tutor frequently disrespects those boundaries, the relationship will quickly deteriorate, and the ability of this particular professional to help the student will plummet accordingly.

Moreover—how is the tutor's demeanor? Is he or she patient as a tutor? That is a very important factor. The slightest demonstration of impatience might negatively affect the student. Such a demonstration could simply be present in the tutor's tone of voice. That alone could be a deal breaker, since it could actually have an impact on the student's confidence level. It might seem like it wouldn't be that big a deal if the tutor simply acts a bit impatient every now and then, but that is something that shouldn't have any place in this type of arrangement. After all, one of the primary reasons students may need a tutor is essentially to boost their confidence level in a certain subject. Therefore, anything that may lead to the exact opposite effect, such as a display of impatience, certainly shouldn't happen and should not be tolerated if it does take place.

Imagine, for instance, a young lady struggling with physics in her junior year of high school. She isn't doing well in the subject and she asks her parents for help—so they hire a tutor. Her confidence level in physics is rock bottom after a couple of bad grades. After a long day at school, she's tired but she has a tutoring session anyway. The professional starts going through a few questions, trying to explain them, but she is struggling to keep up since she's exhausted. The tutor asks her to try a problem, but she doesn't even understand how to begin! The tutor impatiently says, "But I just explained it to you two minutes ago!"—that alone could crush the student's confidence at that point. This is something that definitely should be avoided at all costs! Tutors must be patient.

Building Rapport during Tutoring Sessions—A Waste of Time?

I strongly believe that it is great for the student and the tutor to build rapport. When the two have a good relationship and shared interests, it is a lot easier for the professional to motivate and inspire the student to succeed. Stricter parents may find it odd if, at any given point in a tutoring session, the student and the tutor are chatting about a topic other than the subject at hand. It is true, of course, that both student and tutor should stay primarily focused on the task—covering content—for most of the tutoring session. I would say between 93% to 97% of the time, depending on the way the two interact together, they should be working on content. However, certain cases may demand more time spent on rapport and confidence-building via topics that may sound like unrelated material.

I can already imagine some parents saying, "So you're suggesting that it's ok for students and tutors to chat during a tutoring session that I am paying for? I'm not paying anyone to sit around and chat with my children... I'm paying them to do some hard work!"

If someone were to tell me that, I would say... but hold on a second! There are plenty of occasions in which a tutoring session would seriously benefit from a brief change of topic for the sake of productivity. Imagine, for instance, a student who is seriously struggling in math. His confidence level is very low and he is really struggling to do the work. Moreover, his level of frustration is going through the roof during the tutoring session because he really doesn't understand a specific problem, even after the tutor has explained it a couple of times. If the tutor tries to push the student even further without giving the student a moment to re-focus, chances are that the level of productivity during the session will simply go down the drain. Instead of pushing the student to the verge of sheer desperation, the tutor should wisely take a moment to take the student's attention away from the tough math problem so that he can blow off some steam and regain some traction. The tutor could perhaps ask a question or two about the pupil's day and perhaps even tell a quick joke to lighten things up. Very often, doing so will contribute significantly to the tutoring session's productivity by allowing the student to re-focus and regain some confidence while also further improving the relationship between the student and the tutor. The student might think, "What a good tutor... he totally understood that I was feeling overwhelmed and he briefly took my mind off the problem so I could re-focus."

There are, naturally, parents who will still disagree with me. If you are one of them and you prefer that the sessions have no "chit chat" at all, I would suggest you make that clear to the student and the tutor in advance, so that the expectations are laid on the table and there will be less potential for misunderstandings. That being said, speaking from experience, I have witnessed a great deal of highly successful tutoring engagements develop between productive students and tutors, and many of these engagements included brief casual conversations taking place every now and then. From experience, if the rules of the tutoring sessions are too rigid, the tutoring often won't be as effective as it could be.

Of course, some tutors may overdo it and stay off topic for too long during the tutoring sessions. When that is the case, the issue should certainly be dealt with and brought to the tutor's attention. Saying something to the professional along the lines of the following would usually suffice: "Jake, it is clear that you are doing a good job with Mike, and I have no reason to question your professionalism. However, it seems that you two are getting off topic a bit too often. Please don't let that happen, since Mike really needs to focus."

Looking for a Good Match between Student and Tutor

Now let's explore the topic of finding a good match between a student and a tutor a bit further. Sometimes, it could take several different tries before a student finally finds a tutor that he or she is comfortable working with and can learn well from. Let us assume that a student tries working with several tutors that have a certain skill level—all of them are experienced and skilled at tutoring. Despite their similar skills level, it is very likely that the student will be extremely comfortable working only with a portion of them. Certain students are less picky, but even such students will usually learn more from tutors who have a teaching style that better matches their specific learning style.

For this reason, it is important to find a great match. But how to do so without wasting a lot of time and money?

The "Shotgun Approach"

Ideally, a student could try working with several different tutors within a small period of time in order to select the best possible match. That way, he or she could be exposed to various tutoring methods and quickly find the best tutor for him or her. Many parents and students feel a bit uneasy when this approach is suggested, since they don't feel good about "rejecting" the tutors that aren't selected at the end of the process.

For instance, let's say a student schedules sessions with six different tutors to see if she can find a good match—someone who she feels very comfortable working with. By the end of the six sessions, she decides to work with one of the tutors on a regular basis, but she might feel bad about letting the other five tutors know that she prefers working with someone else. After all, it may almost feel like she needs to fire five different people!

I would argue that as long as everyone is made aware of the process before it takes place, no one should take it personally. Additionally, it is important to stress to the different tutors that the student will select the professional who best matches his or her learning style. When thinking about it that way, it becomes clear that it isn't a matter of who is better or worse as a professional (something that could be taken personally). Instead, it's a matter of fit between a professional's teaching style and a student's learning style.

Let's be realistic here—unless a student tries working with a few different tutors, he or she won't necessarily have a lot of perspective in terms of how great a tutor could be. Let's imagine a student who has only worked with one English tutor throughout her entire academic career. The student and the tutor have built a lot of rapport throughout the years and things always seem to be going well. However, is this tutor really the best available for her? How would she know that if she hasn't tried working with anyone else? It could very well be that if she tried working with a few other tutors, she would actually find that one of the other tutors' approach is more effective than her first tutor's. But of course, she would never find that out unless she tried working with other professionals.

Now let's take a step back for a second. The student would inevitably feel a great degree of loyalty towards her old tutor. She might feel terrible letting her tutor know that she is even considering working with other tutors. What now? Let's explore that in some more detail.

Loyalty in Tutoring—A Closer Look (And How to Move On)

It is natural that once students and tutors build a certain degree of rapport, a good deal of loyalty is developed. That may be true for most professional service relationships in one way or another, but it is especially true in tutoring relationships because there is usually a strong team-like atmosphere that develops once a student and a tutor work together towards the same goal, which is to help the student succeed. It is almost inevitable that a strong bond may develop between a student and a tutor, especially when great results are attained from working together. Because of that, the idea of working with anyone else who may tutor in the same subject might just seem strange and disloyal to the professional.

Chapter 1: Tutoring

There is nothing wrong with a student being loyal to a specific tutor, unless the student and the parents know that they would certainly be better off if they hired someone else... but they don't want to move on due to loyalty.

Where should students and parents draw the line and make the decision to cut ties and start looking for a new tutor? I would say the line should be drawn once the student and the parents can clearly see that the tutor's help is not leading to significant results and everything indicates that nothing will change in this regard. The only issue with this is that these factors are often hard to evaluate. Also, students and parents can often disagree in this regard. When that is the case, it is important for everyone to try to be as objective as possible. If the student has a strong tie with the tutor, but the parents can tell that not enough progress is being made, they need to ask the student to be honest with him or herself. They could ask, for instance, "So, is Mr. Jones really helping you in math as much as you need, or is it that you just can't imagine working with a different tutor because you like him as a person and are used to his approach? I know it may be tough, but this is about your future. Please give this some serious thought!"

Now, how to actually cut ties with the tutor when it becomes clear that it is indeed necessary to move on? I believe that as long as the tutor is given enough notice (for arrangements that have gone on for a long time, perhaps even a month's notice should be considered—otherwise, two weeks should be more than enough), no one really has much of a reason to be upset. In case you want to be extra careful not to hurt the tutor's feelings, the student could let the professional know that it may be a good idea to move on, since overdependence (check our section on "Overdependence on the Academic Team") on any specific tutor's methods can be detrimental for the student in the long run—which is the sheer truth in any case!

Finding a Good Tutor—Local Agencies and Tutoring Businesses

So let's say you are considering hiring a tutor from a local business—I definitely have a few words of advice for you. As a rule of thumb, local tutoring agencies and businesses can be a good place to find great tutors, as long as they are well managed. The longer they have been in business, the better they tend to be.

Many of these organizations are run by passionate education professionals who have a lot of experience in hiring good tutors. When that is the case, all the better. That being said, in many small local tutoring businesses, a common issue arises. You may come across it somewhat often if you do some research, especially in cities with smaller populations: you may find that only one or two of the tutors working at small tutoring businesses are actually great, and that they have extremely busy schedules, while the other professionals are just starting out and don't have the same level of experience or talent as the top tutors. When that is the case, it is still worth trying to work with the less experienced tutors—because you never know, you may find a great professional! However, in case it doesn't work out, feel free to go ahead and firmly request the more experienced tutor's time.

Regardless of who is assigned to work with the student, it is always worth it to inquire about the tutor, no matter how much you trust the organization. You definitely don't need to conduct a full interview, but it is a good idea to learn at least a little about the person. Ask about his or her experience level, academic background, interests and additional jobs. Does he or she seem to be the type of person who can teach and inspire students?

Something else that I believe parents should do when employing a local tutoring business is to inquire about their educational philosophy before getting started. Having a chat with the founder or owner is a good way to get a feeling for how the company operates. Are they the kind of business that is always in a rush to get clients in and out? Or are they passionate people who will do their best to do a great job with each and every student? Parents can usually get a clear picture of what the answers to these questions would be after having a chat with the owner of the small business.

Another thing to watch out for is that many local agencies and tutoring businesses tend to have awkward contracts and rules, so just make sure you understand what they expect you to sign before you get started. For instance, many businesses have extremely strict cancellation policies. I would say that a 24 hour cancellation policy is fair and is an industry standard. However, some places may stretch the cancellation policy a bit further. I have heard of local businesses that would lock parents into contracts that were completely inflexible—their children had to be at the tutoring business's location at certain times every week, and if they failed to make it, even if the tutors were notified weeks in advance, the sessions would be charged to the parents' account. With a cancellation policy that unfair, I would suggest that parents look elsewhere.

Keep in mind that when parents are enrolling their children in a tutoring service, they tend to simply overestimate how disciplined their children may be, especially if the tutoring service comes highly recommended. For example, an hour and a half twice a week may sound like a great idea until the student's soccer season starts. Then, of course, it all becomes a juggling act. The only issue is that if the tutoring business has a really inflexible contract, then parents might end up wasting a lot of money by committing to more than the student(s) can handle.

What about Free Tutoring?

In the past few years, a great deal of programs have become available offering free tutoring—either through government-funded initiatives or, quite simply, specific institutions that have made tutoring accessible for the sake of educating the youth, with the vision of helping to improve society. Many of these initiatives are great and worthy of admiration, since they will likely be able to provide students in need with something that they would otherwise not have available. Now, with these programs available out there, why would anyone pay for tutoring?

I would say that it is for roughly the same reason I often get expensive coffee at various coffee shops instead of free coffee at rest area locations on the highways. The various coffee shops, although more expensive, are more readily available. Also, I can be certain that a specific level of quality will be provided at the expensive coffee shops, while I wouldn't be as confident that I could find the same quality at the rest areas. Moreover, I can get a highly personalized cup of coffee at the various expensive coffee shops, while the same isn't true at the rest areas—there, the only level of personalization I can get with my coffee is sugar and cream.

Putting my analogy aside, one could certainly find great tutors through the free programs available, depending on the availability of such programs wherever one may live. That being said, the quality of the tutoring can often be a hit-or-miss. Additionally, the availability may be restricted or very limited, especially if the program is very popular. Finally, one may only have the luxury of personalization—from the choice of tutors to control over the terms of the whole engagement—when one is actually paying for tutoring.

Of course, if you have free quality tutoring available in your area, you should definitely give it a try for your child. If the student is unable to obtain as much support as he or she needs from the free tutoring program, you can then turn to alternative choices.

Chapter 1: Tutoring

Finding a Good Independent Tutor

Nowadays, there are so many places to go and so many different choices out there that parents can easily get overwhelmed in the search for an independent tutor for their children. Here is a list of where one could potentially get started:

• **School counselors and teachers**. They often know popular local tutors and are usually happy to refer them. Also, most schools have a good "tutor directory".

• **Online tutor directories**. There are quite a few good ones out there with frequently updated listings of tutors all over the world.

• **Your own community**. Often, parents of students around the same age as your child may be able to refer someone who has worked with their children.

• **Classified ads.** Local newspapers often have lots of tutoring ads for independent tutors. Online classifieds, especially free ones, can also have a great reach.

- **Bulletin boards** (community boards as well as local colleges). They very often have postings for tutors of various subjects.

Of course, you can also reach out and post ads yourself. In that case, I would always strongly recommend being extremely cautious—make sure to check additional references and ask for a police background check when you hire someone you met directly from a post or an ad.

One note in case you are reaching out: I have come across a lot of parents who had something specific in mind and showed no willingness to be flexible. In many cases, their requests were for things that were essentially irrelevant. For instance, many parents seem to think that a tutor should have a minimum of five years of experience as a teacher or hold a PhD or some specific certification when in reality, none of these accomplishments should be a minimum requirement. Why is that? Because such requirements will only serve to weed out a great number of potentially fantastic tutors.

For instance, a student's mother reached out to me specifically looking for a tutor currently teaching in the school system who would also have a certain certification that was required (due to her child's learning disability). The latter was, of course, a completely reasonable request. However, the former requirement was completely pointless, and she showed no flexibility in reconsidering it (despite my genuine attempts to try to change her mind, given that I had a fantastic tutor available who didn't meet that specific condition, since she wasn't currently teaching in the school system). Why did she have such a requirement? She believed that the only way for a tutor to be familiar with the school curriculum was for him or her to be currently employed in the school system. Her assumption was, in itself, incorrect. Many a tutor not currently employed in the public school system would have more than enough familiarity with the school curriculum in order to teach her child. So, right off the bat, she narrowed the search significantly with her specific request for a reason that was essentially irrelevant. In fact, by imposing such a restriction, she simply denied her daughter the opportunity of potentially having a fantastic tutor who would very likely have a remarkably positive impact on her academic career.

What Should You Be Flexible about When Hiring a Tutor?

The following requirements are still important and should naturally be considered when selecting a tutor. However, a parent should be flexible when considering them. In other words, these specific requirements don't necessarily need to be deal-breakers.

1st – The tutor's education. Some parents tend to choose the tutor with the highest level of education while often simply disregarding other key characteristics. Think about it: would Johnny, a fifth grade student, really need someone with a PhD to teach him how to add and subtract fractions properly? Of course not. Naturally, many people who hold PhDs could make fantastic tutors, but that's not the point. The point is that the level of education in itself shouldn't be a primary deal-breaker as long as the tutor is educated enough to properly tackle and teach the content.

2nd – The tutor's years of experience. That's another attribute that parents tend to put excessive emphasis on. Of course, experience is important, and a tutor with a lot of experience, all other things being equal, will likely be a better tutor than a tutor with no experience. However, years of experience alone won't tell you the whole story. I have met a tutor, for instance, who claimed to have more than 10 years of experience tutoring all levels of math, but according to two of my students, he was just terrible despite all his experience. So how could we explain that? It actually turned out that his experience was in casual tutoring spread over 10 years while also working at a full-time job.

3rd – Teaching experience. Again, just like in terms of tutoring experience, someone with substantial teaching experience will likely be a better tutor (all other things being equal) than someone without any teaching experience. However, teaching experience alone is no flawless predictor of a tutor's quality. Also, it essentially takes a different set of skills to be a great school teacher than to be great at teaching students privately. Of course, there are many teachers who have it all and are able to excel in teaching individually as well as in classrooms... but that's certainly not always the case.

4th – Price. The most expensive tutor will not always be the best tutor. However, higher prices usually do tend to signal quality.

The Tutor's Hourly Rate—What It Can Tell You

How much can someone infer from a specific tutor's hourly rate? I would say that a tutor who has a higher-than-average hourly rate will often (but not always) be a "better" tutor than someone who charges an average or a below-average hourly rate.

However, there is certainly no guarantee that this would always be the case. And we also need to be careful with the word "better"... After all, what makes a tutor better than any other? One specific student may prefer working with a tutor whom another student finds boring or hard to connect with. The main thought here is that a tutor with a higher rate will often be more experienced and usually more skilled at teaching than a tutor with a lower rate. Additionally, rates are often a function of the general location where a tutor usually works. For instance, if a tutor usually has many clients in an affluent neighborhood, he or she will very likely have a higher rate than another tutor who works in a less affluent area.

So now you could be asking—why may a tutor's higher-than-average rate be a signal of the quality of his or her work? The answer may be obvious to some—after all, that is the case in many other industries—but it's interesting to delve a bit deeper into this topic, especially since pricing in the world of tutoring is a bit exaggerated when facing the usual economics of service businesses... And why is that so? Because tutors provide a very unique service that is extremely important. Whenever the high quality of a specific tutor's work becomes well-known in a certain area, the parents of students who really need the professional's help will be willing to pay a very high price for it. It's not quite the same when we compare tutoring to another service business—like gardening, for instance. Sure, a homeowner can care a lot about his garden, but he will certainly care a lot more about his child's future. Not only that, but most quality garden services will be able to provide a similar result (a nice clean garden)... however, a great tutor's work will be a lot harder to emulate if he has great skills and a good connection with the student.

For those reasons, and due to high demand, education professionals with a lot of skill and experience will often have higher-than-average rates—and sometimes, the variation between the rates among various tutors may differ significantly. However, it is again worthwhile to stress that there are certainly fantastic professionals out there whose rates are not that high. If you are able to find them, try your best to keep them!

Should I Hire a "Cheap" Tutor If I Have a Tight Budget?

Perhaps—depending on the quality of his or her work. If it isn't great, hiring the "cheap" tutor won't turn out to be such a cheap choice. Sometimes, hiring a tutor with a low hourly rate can turn out to be a more costly decision—unless this tutor is actually very talented. But let's assume that a tutor with a low rate isn't that experienced and doesn't have as much talent as another tutor with a higher rate. In that case, a student would likely need a lot more time with the less talented tutor to cover the exact same content that the more talented tutor could cover in less time and also more effectively. Let me illustrate this with a simple example... let's say that Eric charges $60/hour and he is extremely experienced and talented as a tutor. Meanwhile, Bob charges $40/hour and he doesn't have as much experience as Eric. Jayme, a hard-working student, works with Bob for four hours to prepare for her exam, which costs her $160. Unbeknownst to her, Eric is a lot more effective than Bob and he could have prepared her for the same exam in just two and a half hours! Since that would have cost her $150, she could have saved $10 (and an hour and a half—which she could have spent studying more) by working with Eric instead of Bob.

Of course, in reality, it would be hard to evaluate exactly how long it would take for each tutor to go over a specific amount of material with the student. However, after working with different tutors, students will usually have a sense of who they can work better with, and who the most effective tutor would be for them. I would then argue that the most cost-effective way to go about hiring is to work with the most effective tutor—as long as his or her hourly rate is not completely unreasonable.

A Note on the Tutor's Gender, Age and Background

Should the tutor's gender matter? Some students and parents are very particular about the tutor's gender. Often, for younger female students, parents prefer the tutor to be a female, since the student may feel uncomfortable with a male tutor. That is understandable, but there could be plenty of great male tutors who wouldn't make the young student uncomfortable. My suggestion is for parents and students to try to keep an open mind.

The same idea applies to age and background. Of course, some students may connect a lot more easily with younger tutors, but that doesn't mean that it would be impossible for them to connect with an older tutor. Also, a tutor's background shouldn't be a factor in tutor selection at all. If the tutor is from abroad, it's actually neat to have the tutor share his or her experiences with the student and present a new culture to them. Therefore, a tutor's background shouldn't interfere in the selection process whatsoever.

So what should one look for in a tutor?

Let's get started with the most important points:

- Great personality
- Charisma and people skills
- Leadership skills
- Patience
- Passion for teaching
- Enough education/experience
- Excellent references

Needless to say, many of these characteristics are hard to measure objectively. Usually, the student and the parent must be the judges after meeting the tutor in person for the first time.

Also, there are certain "unusual" indicators (which could be found in a tutor's resume and/or cover letter) that often signal desirable characteristics such as charisma, patience, people skills, and leadership. For instance:

- Volunteer work (the more extensive, the better)
- Career options or interest in health care (nursing, medicine, dentistry, etc.)
- Leadership roles in sports activities (team captain, coaching, etc.)

What to Ask from an Independent Tutor

Certainly, and perhaps most importantly, a parent should ask an independent tutor for several references. You want to get a good feel for the impression he or she has left on other people—especially in regard to his or her demeanor. It's a good idea to check at least three references.

What else should you ask an independent tutor? It is fair to request a quick interview in person, especially when the tutor hasn't been referred by someone you know.

Interviewing a Tutor

What to ask in an interview? There are a few great questions (both simple and more complex) that you can choose from for getting acquainted with the tutor's overall philosophy, teaching style, personality, and begin evaluating whether or not the professional would be a good match for the student:

- What's your teaching philosophy?
- How would you describe your teaching style?
- Have your past students often shown improvement? To what extent?
- Do you feel like you can inspire and motivate students? If so, do you have any examples from experience?
- If a student is really struggling with a concept and does not understand it even after you have explained it a couple of times, how do you usually proceed?
- Do you usually prepare prior to tutoring sessions?
- How does the standard tutoring session usually go?

Note that the best thing to do, usually, is to keep the interview somewhat casual. That way, you can have a more genuine feel for the way the tutor will eventually interact with the student. The best tutors will usually be more engaging conversationalists and better able to express themselves. If they are exciting individuals, all the better. Additionally, the interview doesn't have to be extremely long—half an hour should be more than enough.

Online Tutors—Are They a Good Choice?

Online tutoring has started to become popular, and the trend indicates that it will continue to become more and more popular. Online tutoring can be great, but the results will greatly depend on the tutor's skills—even more so than tutoring in person. Why is that? Only a highly skilled and charismatic tutor would be able to engage and inspire a student through the cold screen of a computer monitor. In person, it is usually easier to motivate, engage and inspire.

What about Group Tutoring? Is It a Good Idea?

Many tutoring services and independent tutors offer group tutoring—that is, tutoring with multiple students at a time, usually at a discount. While this type of arrangement may work well on some occasions, I would argue that individual, personalized tutoring will usually lead to a much more positive impact on the student's confidence and level of understanding. Usually, the more personalized the help, the greater the improvement in the student's academic performance.

In some cases, if a student has a friend or two who also need tutoring at a similar level, then it could potentially be a good idea—depending on a variety of factors. It would be fundamental for the students to be able to work well together while not getting distracted, which is something that is hard to evaluate. How can parents evaluate the group's productivity on a regular basis unless they are present during the sessions? It is indeed challenging. And of course, if the students are getting together for the group tutoring sessions and frequently spending a lot of time chatting about unrelated topics, the whole experience would be a complete waste of time for everyone involved.

Interestingly enough, even the most disciplined and hard-working students may change in a group setting. Consequently, it's not enough to make a decision either way on the basis of how hard-working the students usually are. In a group setting, they may just take a step back, act more social and not work nearly as hard as they would if they were to have individual tutoring sessions instead.

Chapter 1: Tutoring

Finding a Good Tutor on a Budget

As we have previously discussed, a tutor's hourly rate won't reflect the real cost of tutoring since it doesn't take a tutor's effectiveness into account. In the example we used, a tutor with a cheaper hourly rate actually turned out to be more expensive than a tutor who charged a higher rate but was more effective, since fewer hours were employed by the latter in order to cover the same amount of material—ultimately leading to a lower cost. Now, let's further discuss how to find a good tutor on a budget.

So where to start for parents on a budget? How can parents find good professionals who are willing to work for less? The first idea is simple: at least initially, focus on looking for and hiring less experienced professionals. The only issue is that since their level of skill and experience isn't always sufficient, the quality of their work may not necessarily be the best. Of course, more experienced professionals with long track records of success will usually charge a lot more than young and talented college students or recent graduates, for instance, with less tutoring experience. Every now and then, however, parents may be able to find excellent young professionals to support students at a very reasonable cost. That being said, in order for that to fall into place, usually both patience and luck are required. Often, it will take a few tries to find a great match when using this approach.

In case parents decide to try finding a good professional with less experience, I would suggest they go into the search process without expecting to find the perfect match right away. Get started with the willingness to go through a couple of disappointments so that no one gets frustrated. In order to expedite the process, parents can try the "shotgun approach" and set up sessions with several young professionals within a short period of time. That way, the chances of finding a good match are substantially increased.

It is very important to note that in today's society, there are a large number of young professionals available and willing to work for reasonable amounts of money. Patient parents who are willing to put effort into the hiring process may be able to put an excellent team into place for their children, formed primarily of young and somewhat inexperienced (yet still talented) professionals at a very low cost.

To sum it all up, there is usually a bit of a trade-off between money and time, combined with effort, when looking for great tutors. Of course, note that none of these factors would actually guarantee great tutoring without an element of luck added to the mix. However, parents who are willing to spend more money on tutoring may find highly skilled professionals more quickly than otherwise. If they do not wish to invest as much money, parents would usually need to spend more time and effort looking for a great tutor who charges less.

CHAPTER 2: THE ACADEMIC TEAM

Chapter 2: The Academic Team

An academic team? So students may need more than just tutors? So what's an academic team and who needs one?

An academic team is a group of dedicated individuals who provide personalized support to a student on a regular or semi-regular basis. It can consist of tutors, mentors, educational consultants, coaches and counsellors, among other professionals. Throughout this book, we are usually going to refer to academic team members as those professionals who work with the student (primarily) on an individual basis. Thus, whenever we refer to "the academic team," I won't mean to include the student's school teachers, for instance, unless they also work with them regularly on a one-on-one basis. Now, this may sound exaggerated to some parents; why would one particular student need a group of people for academic support unless he or she has "something wrong" with him or her? The answer is simple: competition—just as I mentioned when arguing in favour of tutoring. The stakes have never been higher, and competition has never been as widespread or as strong. For top college programs, competition has never been fiercer and requirements for acceptance keep going through the roof.

Note that some students will require only one or two professionals, while others may require a few

Chapter 2: The Academic Team

more. Naturally, the gap between a student's current level and what his or her goals are will determine the size and caliber of the academic team that is required. A small team may be sufficient for a student who is close to reaching his or her goals. Conversely, if the gap between where the student is currently at and where he or she needs to be is very large, the team will likely need to be more impressive in order to support the student in reaching his or her goals.

Parents have the power to handpick a strong team that can assist the student in reaching his or her highest goals. It's tempting to try to stick with the brave (and somewhat romantic) idea of letting students do it all on their own. But since competition is usually hiring the best of the best in preparing them to reach their goals, it becomes challenging for students who don't have the same level of support—even when they are very gifted and have fantastic work habits.

I know what you might be thinking at this point, "Well, what is that going to cost me? Putting a team together is undoubtedly going to cost me an arm and a leg!" That isn't necessarily the case. Nowadays, there are a lot of great professionals who price their services very reasonably. Additionally, there are a lot of programs available that offer either free tutoring or free mentoring, making top people available to help students achieve their goals.

The ideal team will support the student's academic needs while greatly increasing the student's level of motivation and confidence. Additionally, it will empower the student and inspire him or her to work as hard as possible and to reach for the stars. But in order for these great things to occur, of course, the student needs to be very willing to work with the team and must look up to all its individual members, which is something we will discuss in detail.

So let's get started by looking at the different roles that could be present in a great academic team.

Introducing the Main Roles within an Academic Team

For now, let's forget about job "titles" such as mentors, tutors, consultants, counselors, etc... Let's focus on the practical and psychological roles present in a great academic team. In other words, we are going to focus on the main individual roles that should be present within an ideal team. Please note that it is possible for an individual to perform more than one role. For instance, a particular tutor could perform the role of a subject expert and motivator, as long as he or she is good at both. Needless to say, some people are usually naturally better suited to perform certain roles, and often it doesn't take too long for professionals to reveal their strengths in their work.

Before we go into more detail exploring each different role, let us briefly introduce each one of them:

The Subject Expert

The subject expert will support the student with subject content, whether a student is struggling or if he or she just needs added reinforcement in order to remain on top of things. Naturally, if the student needs support with more than one subject, he or she may require more than one subject expert. Tutors or teachers that are able to assist the student on a one-on-one basis would qualify as subject experts. Needless to say, it is important for them to be very knowledgeable with the course's content.

The Motivator

The motivator should inspire and boost the confidence of the student, so he or she must be someone with great energy and charisma. However, there is no need for a professional motivational speaker; all a student really needs is someone who can build rapport and trust with the ability to inspire. It would be worthless if an enthusiastic motivator couldn't build trust with the student, since in that case, his or her words would fall on deaf ears.

It is ideal, but not required, for the motivator to have some level of authority within the academic sphere. Why? Well, imagine a football coach without any knowledge of mathematics telling a student that he greatly believes that he or she can succeed at math. Surely, the student may feel good about the vote of confidence, but probably won't be completely sold.

Sure, great motivators may have a fantastic impact on the student's level of confidence, which could eventually translate into a positive effect across all areas. However, it is rare for motivators to have such a remarkable overall effect. Needless to say, that usually doesn't happen overnight.

The Planner

The planner will help the student look at the big picture and lay down a foundation for a solid game plan—a design that will empower the student in his or her quest for academic success. The importance of planning is often overlooked; especially since many students often don't have an idea of what they want to do in the future in terms of a career, which in turn leads some to believe that short or long-term planning isn't beneficial before figuring out what they want to pursue. Even for students who have a clear picture of their future goals, present challenges often make long-term planning seem less important. However, planning usually makes a really positive difference and gives students a sense of direction, a sense of mission. Planning doesn't have to take place as regularly as motivational or instructional work, but its importance is still dramatically high.

The Discipline Coach

The discipline coach may have the hardest role of all: his or her job is to keep the student's discipline in check and support the student in becoming efficient and organized. It may not be fun but the importance thereof should be self-explanatory. Ideally the coach will have a great relationship with the student and will have a keen sense of where the student's limits lie. Of course, the student's limits can and should be pushed every once in a while, but often their boundaries need to be respected.

The greater the level of rapport between the coach and the student, the better. Needless to say, the student also needs to have great respect for the professional and preferably look up to him/her.

The type of coach will also depend on the student's personality. Some students can greatly benefit from working with a very strict coach, while others would have better results with the exact opposite—someone who can enforce discipline more tactfully. A personality mismatch can often lead to complete chaos, so the choice of coach deserves a good deal of careful contemplation.

Forming the Team with All Different Roles

As mentioned before, one specific person could perform more than one role. In some cases, you may also need more than one team member sharing the same role. Imagine, for instance, a team with two or three great motivators; that would be (arguably) enough to inspire any student.

The parent, then, usually has the role of team manager, allocating available time and resources to put together the best possible team. Needless to say, gathering the perfect team will take good intuition, management skills, patience and a little luck. However, a great team can have a remarkably positive effect on students' level of success, leading them to realize their true potential.

Naturally, since all students are different, the ideal team for one student may look very different compared to the ideal team for another. For instance, students with lower levels of confidence will need strong motivators and instructors. Students who are a bit disorganized may need great discipline coaches, and so on. An important part of the process of putting a team in place is to determine what the student's needs are. In order to do so, parents may have to rely on opinions coming from various professionals in order to get a real feel for what kind of support the student really requires.

More on the topics of recognizing needs, evaluating professionals, reaching out and putting the team together can be found under "Developing the Perfect Academic Team—The System."

Getting the Student On Board with Getting Help

Now, let's get to something pretty important, which is getting the student on board with having an academic team to support them and also meeting the various professionals on a regular basis. What if you're willing to give this a try but the student is reluctant, even if just a little bit? So let's pretend that he or she tells you:

Chapter 2: The Academic Team

"What? You're paying for some random person to tutor me/motivate me/plan my future/help me with discipline? Thanks, but no thanks! You can keep your money!"

How can you change the student's mind? Of course, our strategies should also work for students that aren't as radical.

One important thing to stress at this point is that I am, by no means, an expert on parenting. In that area, you are the expert. With that in mind, the following tips and strategies have been collected from several fantastic parents of students who I have worked with, who have kindly agreed to share what have been the most successful strategies for them, along with the added perspective of the students' psychological standpoints. These aren't necessarily the reinvention of the wheel, but I am confident that going through them will, at the very least, give parents good ideas on how to get students on board.

So without further ado, here are our most popular strategies:

1st – Incentives. Ok, I'm not necessarily a huge fan of this one, but let's be honest here…it often works. Sometimes, it may be the parents' only choice in case the student is being particularly stubborn. How about this: you can offer them something small in exchange for just one try, that is, for them to meet the person once and see how it goes. Very often, that one try is all it will take for the student to get on board. If it doesn't work, you can ask the student a few questions and more often than not, become successful the second or third time around. In case you are morally against bribery, that's ok, of course you can try different strategies instead.

2nd – A casual meeting. How about inviting the person over for dinner so you can casually introduce him or her to the student? If the professional is an interesting person (hopefully that's actually the case), chances are that most students will more easily warm up to the idea of working with him or her. Just remember, someone you may find interesting won't necessarily be interesting to your children. Also, just beware that if the main purpose of the meeting isn't made clear to the student from the very beginning (this is worth mentioning, although most of you are certainly already well aware of it), many young people tend to become resentful when they feel manipulated, and the casual invitation for dinner may appear like an underhanded way for parents to convince their children to get on board with their plan. Therefore, it will usually pay off to be open with your plans right from the start, although that may meet more resistance in some cases.

3rd – Engage the student, including him or her in the decision process. Once you have applicants, or perhaps just certain people in mind, ask your child for his or her opinion on who may be the best option. Even if they reject all alternatives presented, chances are they will be more open and you may get priceless feedback on what they would actually look for in someone to work with. I can already hear some parents' thoughts: "I know exactly what kind of person my child enjoys working with." Ok! That may be the case, but I'd certainly suggest that you keep an open mind. Speaking from experience, a lot of parents I've worked with have often been mistaken in this regard.

4th – A heartfelt conversation. This one, of course, is a no-brainer. The parent can simply sit down with the student and open up, share the idea, and directly convince the student to get on board.

I came up with a little script built on feedback from real students and real parents, which could be changed around depending on your individual needs/thoughts. You could get started with something like:

"I found (or am looking for) someone to work with you on a somewhat regular basis as long as you're on board...he/she will be a pretty neat person and (insert all common interests that the professional has or will have with the student, also fun facts, and accomplishments). I think this would be great, and it's all for your success. He/she is an (insert job title here: academic coach, motivator, planner, or other)—someone who can share their experience in academics with you. You remember Alexander the Great, from your history class? Yeah, the Macedonian king who basically conquered the whole world back then, remember him? He had an academic coach/tutor—and a pretty good one, actually. It was Aristotle, the Greek philosopher. This isn't because I don't believe you're not able to succeed on your own, I believe you are. However, this can just give you a great boost and get you closer to all the things you want to achieve!"

Now, of course, you can change the tone according to what you'd find most appropriate. Naturally, you can find an example other than Alexander the Great. I bet all great people in history, whether ancient history or modern history, have had a great coach, tutor, or mentor. Of course, not all of them necessarily academic, but that's beside the point.

Now, before we move on, just a quick note regarding chatting with your children about their future: Several teenage students that I've taught said it's sometimes painfully awkward to have a conversation with their parents regarding their future. That may not be the case in your family, and if so, that's great! Nevertheless, I've lost count of how many well-intentioned parents I've met who fell into the trap of losing ground with their children whenever their expectations didn't exactly line up with the students' ambitions. I would say that's about the time when things start getting a bit awkward. I've also lost count of how many times I've heard students say, "My mom/dad really wants me to be a (fill in the blank – doctor, lawyer, accountant, etc.), but I really don't want that at all." And the funny thing is that this wasn't actually the truth in many cases; the student was often just under the mistaken impression that this is what the parent(s) actually wanted. For parents who fear that may be the case with their children, I would suggest taking a step back and reminding the child of how they, in the end, just really care about their success.

5th – Some or all of the above strategies combined. I would suggest that you mix and match to try things out. After you employ a few of these strategies, my guess is that you will be able to get almost any student on board, especially if you give it some time (whenever necessary) and allow the student to give his or her input.

Chapter 2: The Academic Team

Important Note: The Title of a Professional & Student Reluctance

Something that I have found quite interesting when helping certain students is that some are reluctant to meet a professional if their title (and role) sounds a bit unusual or unclear to them. For instance, let's say that you tell your child that you are hiring a "discipline coach" for her, since you believe she would greatly benefit from a few sessions with one. She might immediately act defensive since she hasn't even heard of a "discipline coach" before. She might think or say: "None of my friends have ever worked with one of these, so why on earth would I need to work with one?" However, if you framed things in a different way, both the job title as well as the ultimate goal of the sessions, she will likely be a lot more open.

Not to mention that the student may feel like the sessions are a complete waste of time unless the goals and potential benefits are clearly set. Using the example above once again, the student may think that getting together with someone for the sole purpose of improving their level of discipline would be silly, and that they should instead spend more time studying or doing homework. Of course there are exceptions to this—especially when students need a great deal of assistance in a certain area and are well aware of this fact. When that is the case, they will certainly be a lot more open. But let's consider a situation in which the student still doesn't see the purpose of meeting with a professional with a specific role.

So how could a parent go about reframing the roles in such a way that will make the student willing to work with the professionals? Simple: The easiest way would be to hire the professionals from the team as tutors. After all, tutors are "accepted" by students in almost every single social circle. The only challenge lies in finding tutors who will be able to help the student with a specific subject (that the student needs help with) and who can also be great at performing specific roles (motivator, planner, or discipline coach).

Once the professional relationship is set up and the tutoring sessions are already taking place, the tutor and the student can agree to work on specific issues unrelated to the subject at hand during pre-determined periods of time. For instance, the chemistry tutor and the student can work on chemistry for an hour, and thereafter focus on discipline and organization for another half hour.

Taking a Closer Look at the Four Main Roles

The Role of the Subject Expert

This is the role most parents are already quite familiar with, since (as we have already mentioned before) the subject expert is essentially either a tutor or a teacher who works with the student on a frequent basis. Given that the topic of tutoring has already been covered in this book, we will not go over it in much further detail under this section. That being said, it is still worthwhile to explore the scope of the role, as well as discuss the possibility of having tutors who play various roles within the academic team.

Let's then get started with the scope of a subject expert's responsibilities. Students will need these professionals to give them the support they require for performing well in specific subjects. Naturally, in order to provide proper support to a student in a given subject, the professional needs to have a strong grasp of the specific subject, at least up to the level of the student's current course. Almost needless to say, the professional also must be able to teach the student in a clear way and to do so with confidence. Additionally, the professional must be able to think quickly on his or her feet and answer questions as they arise. Moreover, the subject expert should also have the skill to engage the student while directing the course of the session with the goal to (occasionally) challenge the student, and to lead him or her to become more confident in the course.

Can a subject expert also be a motivator, a planner or a discipline coach (in case he or she proves to be talented at it)? Most certainly. However, it is ideal for each subject expert to spend time with the student primarily on the specific topic, and perform the additional role separately. For example, if a math tutor also does a great job of helping the student develop discipline and get organized, he or she can perform the role of discipline coach in addition to tutoring (ideally not taking time away from the required support in math). The professional can also potentially set up extra sessions with the sole purpose of focusing on discipline.

Keep in mind that while you may be able to find someone who is good at both being a subject expert for a specific course and playing a different role (motivator, discipline coach, etc.), it is likely you will find two different people who are individually better at each task than one person who is tackling both things at once. The key is to really identify each professional's strengths. It is not that easy to find professionals who are going to be amazing as subject experts and also be fantastic at other roles.

Of course there are great exceptions to this. Sometimes it becomes evident that a specific subject expert is actually able to do two things very well—for instance, tutor students in a given subject while greatly motivating them and potentially also developing their discipline. Often, professionals who can indeed play two or more roles really well show characteristics of being polymaths. Imagine, for instance, an educational professional with an accomplished music background who also has a Master's Degree in mathematics and speaks several languages. Such a polymath would likely also be capable of performing multiple roles within the academic team, since a wide variety of skills usually signals competence in a wide variety of areas. Please note that this observation comes from experience; many multi-talented tutors I hired and worked with in the past were able to perform more than one role extremely well in students' academic teams.

Ensuring the Professional is a Good Match

A professional's level of mastery over the subject at hand is actually completely irrelevant if he or she can't teach it well. More specifically, it is paramount that all subject experts are good matches for the students they are working with. Students need to feel confident that the professionals are able to teach them in a way that they can understand.

Aside from a basic connection and a good personality matchup, there must also be a good match between the way the expert teaches and the student's learning style. Too commonly, the importance of this match in style is ignored. For instance, let's say a student tells her parents after a couple of sessions that she wasn't able to follow everything that was taught by the tutor (who had been highly recommended). Her parents may feel tempted to assume that she simply didn't focus hard enough throughout the lesson.

It's important to remember that a highly recommended subject expert won't necessarily be the perfect fit for every single student out there, so let us always keep in mind the importance of finding professionals who will match well with the student. By ensuring we have a great match, the student's results can improve significantly in a shorter period of time.

The Role of the Motivator

Before we introduce the role in itself, let's consider this question: So what's effective in terms of student motivation? In other words, what are the most powerful and effective ways in which a professional can engage students and lead them to success?

Building a great connection with students is highly effective. However, just building that connection isn't enough—the person must also be assertive and preferably successful in the eyes of the student. Moreover, this individual should be able to relate to the pupil and inspire him or her to work hard while showing that if there is a will, there is a way. The professional should be someone who will make the student feel more confident than they have ever been, eventually leading him or her to believe that their dreams are attainable through hard work and perseverance.

But let's start from the beginning: How could anyone find someone with the ability to do what we just described? At this point, it may sound too good to be true. Who could realistically make these fantastic things happen?

The Common Interests Shared by a Student and a Motivator

A motivator should be someone with at least one (preferably more) genuine interest in common with the student, combined with leadership skills. So, what could this shared interest be? Anything, really;

a specific sport or activity, and the narrower, the better. For example, let's pretend little Nancy is obsessed with dancing and has been doing ballet since she was two years old. Imagine if she gets a tutor who danced ballet professionally for a few years and who also turns out to have a great personality. Well then, chances are that little Nancy would likely connect with her new tutor (who will also play the role of motivator).

Note: beware of a few things here...

1st — young people's interests can come and go quickly and completely unannounced. So maybe little Nancy's mom thought she still liked ballet when she was actually fed up with it and in fact, for some strange reason, little Nancy actually recently started despising professional ballet dancers. Wow—you didn't see that coming, right? The point is—we just never know and the funny thing is that parents often think they do know.

2nd — the "common interest approach" is, of course, no true guarantee of rapport between the student and the professional. However, having one great interest in common with the student will greatly boost the chances of the professional establishing great rapport with the student, let alone if there is more than one interest that they share!

Chapter 2: The Academic Team

So...let's move on and talk a bit about leadership skills. I would strongly advise parents to build a team with at least one professional who has great leadership skills. Why? A great leader can have a tremendous positive impact on the academic success of a student.

Imagine a major sports star coming up to your child and saying, "Hey kid, I believe in you. I truly believe you can do anything. Get out there and make it happen." Wow, wouldn't that be something? Ok, I realize not many major sports stars are readily available to go around inspiring young students in person on a regular basis, but I hope you get my point. We can only dream, right?

Finding Great Motivators in Real Life

Let's bring it down a notch (back to reality). Imagine a recent graduate of a well-recognized college who has brought his sports team to great success as its captain. In addition to that, he has also been the president of a couple of his college's minor associations. Now you might think: Great, but how on earth would he be available to work with young students in any way? He's probably on his way to playing professional sports somewhere, or he has probably landed some fantastic job already. Well, I wouldn't doubt either option, but I would argue that there is a very good chance that this person, or someone very much like him, is actually looking for a decent-paying part-time job as he transitions from graduation to professional school, or he might be gearing up to land his dream job in a couple of years.

Nowadays, it's not surprising to find great talent available, especially since the rising tutoring industry offers young professionals an opportunity to engage in a highly rewarding and noble activity that will help young students, while being able to charge more than they would be making on an hourly basis working at many other places. But now you might ask me, "Ok great, but what if this fictitious person in reality is only able to tutor a subject that my son or daughter doesn't need help with?" Simple! You can hire him as an independent motivator (we will go over the job description in the next section).

Of course the role of the motivator can be performed by someone who also takes another professional role in a student's academic team as long as they are talented at it (and it will be the parents' or the student's task to make that determination). Perhaps you are already employing a tutor who is a fantastic motivator. If that is the case, you may not need to hire someone simply to perform this role. However, in case you do not have someone in place who may be able to truly inspire

Chapter 2: The Academic Team

the student, then I would strongly suggest that you start looking for an independent motivator; someone in the academic team whose primary role will be to motivate the student.

Now let's talk about the title of the position of an independent motivator. The word "motivator" itself won't usually sound too appealing to the student. However, I will usually refer to the position throughout this book using the same name, since it will invoke what one of the primary roles of this person will be; which is, of course, to motivate the student. Yet, naturally, that doesn't mean you need to do the same when you are speaking with the student or hiring an individual. I have a few alternative suggestions for the title of the position and you can select any of them, or change them in case you feel creative. How about "academic coach" (or perhaps just "coach"), "academic mentor", "educational consultant", or "student support agent"? They might sound vague and general but that is deliberate—after all, the position itself, in terms of what it should encompass, ought to be somewhat flexible.

The Job Description of an Independent Motivator

At this point, let's say you are searching for the professional (assuming you don't find a subject-specific tutor that would qualify) and you need a job description. That is, of course, assuming that you are not hiring someone who already offers this kind of service and also that you aren't hiring a tutor who will also play the role of a motivator. It's worth noting that in the field of education, consulting is a very broad term nowadays, so you may be able to find someone who does roughly what we are suggesting here and even offers additional services. That being said, it is also fair (and perhaps fun) for you as a parent to have a larger degree of control over what services you want to pay for. So you can take our following suggestion and make changes according to your specific needs:

"Academic Coach required for student support on a semi-regular basis.

"Flexible hours – schedule TBD.

"Previous experience with youth required, along with great references. Additionally, a minimum of a Bachelor's Degree (or equivalent) is required or preferred. Preference will be given to candidates with proven leadership skills (displayed through sports, work experience or related activities).

"The successful candidate will provide guidance and support to an ambitious student during sessions ranging from forty-five minutes to an hour at a time. The successful candidate will ideally be able to build rapport with the student and further inspire him/her to achieve his/her potential by sharing strategies to succeed in academics, while exploring and addressing the student's areas of weakness."

How much should you offer to pay? I would say within the range of whatever academic tutors charge in your area, in case you are hiring someone who doesn't do this type of work on a regular basis already.

Now, I can already imagine hearing some parents asking me, "Ok, so you want me to pay some person to come and hang out with my child and share some ideas on how to succeed in school? That sounds like a waste of money!" Well, if that's you, here is my answer:

First, you can actually go ahead and try to get someone who would do it for free. There are great programs available out there that offer mentorship programs for children. However, as I have suggested before, that will often take away your control over the arrangement. Additionally, in terms of quality, getting something for free is frequently hit-or-miss. You may be able to find someone fantastic but the search may take a lot longer. Chances are that you will likely be able to find a higher quality of service faster if you pay for it.

Second, when properly set up, this sort of engagement that we are suggesting can have an everlasting, remarkably positive impact on your child's life. So I would strongly suggest to sceptical parents to give it a try before making any judgement calls. <u>The risk is minimal</u>—basically, the cost of a single session. Then, in case you still find that there is no value in this type of arrangement, which I would estimate to be about 2 to 3% of parents in total (maybe more in case they can't find the "right" person to do the job), then you can simply tell the person you hired that you just don't think it will work, end of story! So what if you "wasted" $30 or $40 in a genuine attempt to contribute to your child's success?

Setting Up the "Motivation Coach" Sessions and Getting Feedback from the Student

So now let's assume that the student is on board AND that you found someone who you think will be great as a motivator. Before you set up a first session, I suggest you have a chat with the professional to clarify expectations and also to get a feel for how he/she envisions the relationship to work. That way, you have the opportunity to suggest changes accordingly. At this point, it is also good to get an idea of their educational philosophy.

Then you can go ahead and arrange the first session and keep your fingers crossed, hoping it goes well and that the student enjoys the session.

Then, after the session, the moment of truth: ask the student how things went. What we're really hoping for, at this point, is to witness a certain degree of excitement. If there is none, then try to dig a bit deeper to find out how things went and if you think the student can still somehow get engaged and benefit from the experience. If the student is still on board, then set up a second session. Pull the plug if the student still doesn't show any degree of excitement after the second session (perhaps wait for a third session in case the student is usually a tough nut to crack with other activities as well). So if it didn't work with a particular person, I would suggest the rinse and repeat method until you find the right professional. Whatever you do, don't give up too easily before trying the persuasion methods we already went over.

Frequency of Motivational Sessions

Now let's say that the student did actually show excitement after the first couple of sessions. How frequently should you set up the academic coaching/motivational sessions? I would say it greatly depends on the student's needs—and both the student and parents can make that judgment. For instance, if the student is going through a somewhat rough phase, maybe set up weekly or bi-weekly sessions to boost the student's confidence level. On the other hand, if the student is going through a good phase, monthly sessions could suffice.

The Role of the Planner

The planner will support the student as he or she looks ahead. That should include assistance with the student's choices of post-secondary programs and institutions, potential career choices and just simply overall periodical (e.g. term-to-term) planning for the sake of prioritizing.

The required background of the professionals who can perform this role depends on the student's specific needs at the time. For instance, very young students may require simple periodic planning, which would not take a great degree of specialization or knowledge on the part of the planner. Almost any good educational professional who can connect with students and help them with getting things prioritized could potentially perform this specific task well. On the other hand, more specific tasks will require more specialization and knowledge. For instance, if students require a professional who can assist them in the selection of a college program, the best suited person would very likely need to be an educational consultant with a strong background as a school counsellor (or equivalent).

The importance of the planner's role naturally increases dramatically during the student's later years of high school and also in the first years of college as they start looking at various choices for their future. The issue is that, very often, students only start seeking out professional planners when it may already be a little too late. For instance, imagine a student in his senior year of high school hires a consultant who works as an educational consultant in order to assist him with his choice of college. Then, during the meeting he realizes that for the colleges and programs of his choice, he was actually supposed to complete specific courses in his junior year that he, in fact, did not take. As a result, his hands are tied and he would then need to settle for alternative choices, since it would be too late to complete the required courses for his top choices. Needless to say, it would have been greatly beneficial to meet with a planner a couple of years earlier.

Finding the Right Consultant for the Role

In order to find the best possible professional, it is important to make sure that he or she has the right level of expertise to assist the student. The more specific the student's needs, the more care and research one should put into looking for the right professional.

For instance, in case the student is looking for something specific, such as help in determining what courses he or she needs to take in order to apply for specific colleges, look for consultants who have the background and knowledge to assist with that. Does the professional have a background in counseling? Is he or she knowledgeable about the requirements of the colleges the student is interested in? Is this his or her actual area of expertise? These are the types of questions you may want to consider when searching for a professional.

On the other hand, if a student requires a planner for a less specific and more "casual" goal, one can be less picky regarding the professional's expertise and background. For instance, if the professional is only required to get together with the student every three months to discuss what to focus on while considering long-run goals, he or she certainly won't need years of experience to do a great job.

The Role of the Discipline Coach

As we mentioned before, this may be the toughest of the four roles we have presented. The discipline coach should support students in staying disciplined, focused and organized.

Now, for the sake of clarity, let us restrict our definition of the discipline coach's role: he or she should assist the student in developing and maintaining discipline primarily in the academic sphere. That will then exclude sports coaches from our definition, unless they also work with the students on the side, specifically with academics. However, it is also worthwhile to note that most good sports coaches would actually make (equally as) good discipline coaches.

The Ideal Discipline Coach

The ideal discipline coach needs to be strict while maintaining a great relationship with the student. For that reason, he or she will need to be confident and charismatic; someone who can ideally connect with students and make them understand the importance of discipline, determination, and hard work in the pursuit of success and excellence in academics.

Naturally, not many students enjoy being bossed around or told how to get organized or disciplined. Of all the roles, the discipline coach is the most "commanding," something that many students, especially in their teenage years, often feel like rebelling against. Consequently, in order to build their relationship with students while being as strict as necessary, discipline coaches must be tactful. For that reason, discipline coaches need significant people skills in order to make this possible and to understand the student's psychology, including their limits, on a deep level.

As we mentioned before, successful sports coaches (both current and retired) will often make good discipline coaches. Additionally, educational professionals with a background in the military or martial arts will also often be good at performing this role as long as they also have the charisma to complement their skill set.

What Should the Ideal Discipline Coaching Sessions Look Like?

In case they are set as independent sessions, they could be thirty to forty-five minutes in length, taking place on a biweekly basis or more frequently when required. The student and the coach should go over current academic challenges that the student might be facing and go over strategies on how to tackle them. The coach should suggest different activities that should be performed, along with strategies and tips to develop habits that will be useful throughout the student's academic career.

Naturally, the student should see the value in having the sessions and be fully on board with them. Ideally, the students should also enjoy having the sessions. After all, when they don't, all sorts of excuses will be used to try and avoid them at all costs.

Walking the Fine Line—Strengthening Their Relationship with the Student

As we have already alluded to, there's a fine line between developing and maintaining a good relationship with students and being strict enough to truly instill discipline in them. Discipline coaches will be walking that fine line throughout the course of their professional relationship with their students. Consequently, it is important for the professional to be able to show the student all the benefits associated with discipline, determination, and organization. These skills, which need to be carefully honed if a student wants to achieve the highest levels of success, are often overlooked by today's often rebellious youth. Consequently, the discipline coach also needs to be persuasive in getting the students on board with the idea of developing them.

Discipline coaches who are able to develop a strong bond with the student will usually be significantly more successful in getting the student to stay on track and become highly disciplined. The more the student respects and admires the discipline coach, the easier his or her task will become.

The Difference between the Motivator and the Discipline Coach

At this point, you may have noticed some similarities between the two roles. Ideally, both roles need to be filled by charismatic professionals who can connect with the students on a deep level. In a way, both professionals also need to be inspirational. However, I would draw the distinction between the two at the level of their ultimate goals. Ultimately, the discipline coach's goal will be for the student to develop a good level of discipline while staying focused and not letting distractions interfere with their work. On the other hand, the motivator's primary goal is to boost the student's confidence, inspire them, and convince them to shoot for the stars.

Needless to say, there are people out there who could play both roles at once. Great leaders would be able to both inspire and instil a great deal of discipline while strengthening their relationship with their subjects. However, it will often be a lot easier to find two different people who can play each specific role very well.

Chapter 2: The Academic Team

Leading Students versus "Babying" Them

Well, this difference is indeed critical and not all professionals are able to distinguish between leading and babying a student. At a certain age, as all parents probably know, many young individuals gain autonomy and start trying to avoid being "babied" at all costs. Such students (and they do form a very large part of the student population) simply won't respond to a professional who has a condescending tone, and if they do respond, they will do so defiantly. All academic team members must be conscious of that, and if you do hire someone who isn't, the experience can be completely fruitless.

Strictness has a time and place, and although we suggest that whoever plays the role of "discipline coach" when the student needs a certain level of strictness, he or she needs to build and maintain rapport with the student. There is certainly no quicker way for a professional to undermine the relationship with a student than actually being condescending and overly strict. Each student's responsiveness and tolerance level to this kind of approach is different, and it is the professional's responsibility to make sure he or she understands the student.

Developing the Perfect Academic Team: "the System"

We will break down the academic team's development process into a few steps: Recognizing needs, setting a framework for the team, evaluating professionals, reaching out (hiring), and managing.

Recognizing Needs

Looking at the four types of roles we have discussed, which correspond directly to the different needs that a student may have in order to evolve, one must assess what the most important ones are for each student. Does the student need support in specific subjects? Does the student need to become more motivated? Does the student need help planning? And finally, does the student need more discipline in order to succeed? Now, the key will be to identify and recognize those needs and they won't always be that obvious.

That being said, it is very important to note that parents often have a very clear, yet not always accurate, picture of what the student needs. Parents tend to oversimplify the needs of the student, given that they are usually on the outside looking in. This is because they do not (usually) work with their children in an academic environment. Therefore,

Chapter 2: The Academic Team

most the parents' understanding of their children's academic needs arise from past (often early childhood) experiences and parent-teacher meetings, which won't always reveal every student's true needs. Why is that? Even with the best and most dedicated teachers out there, how could they possibly have a deep understanding of all of their students' academic needs? Imagine if a teacher has fifty students. Will he or she have the time and the opportunity to work with all of those students frequently on a one-on-one basis? Most likely not. So most of the teacher's understanding of each student's academic needs will arise from their perceptions of the pupils during class time, which won't always be enough for an in-depth picture. Consequently, a teacher will usually only have significant, deep insight into any particular student's challenges and needs in certain cases. For instance, if they have worked together on a one-to-one basis or if the student is very active in class, the teacher may have a deep and clear understanding of a specific student's needs.

Still, any teacher with whom the student has a strong connection should also be carefully considered in this evaluation. In such cases, why not get together with the teacher to get some feedback and insight on how to bring the student to the next level?

Now, how could parents further determine their children's academic needs? Ideally, they should really gather information from as many educational professionals as possible (including teachers, tutors, counselors, principals, and consultants), especially the ones who have worked with the students on a one-on-one basis most recently, when applicable.

Almost needless to say, the opinion of qualified professionals such as specialized psychologists would be of great value in helping us evaluate the academic needs of a student. Only a few visits could provide tremendous insight into the real academic needs of a child.

It might also be a good idea to ask students about their own needs, although they won't necessarily always know exactly what they are. The greatest problem with this would lie in dealing with students who may get defensive when asked about their challenges, since they would prefer to try to handle them on their own. In that case, it is important to try to lower the student's guard before moving on.

After doing all the research, it will be time to consider overlaps in opinion regarding the student's needs. In some cases they will be obvious, and in other cases not nearly as much. Either way, try your best to prioritize on the basis of what can potentially benefit the student the most.

Chapter 2: The Academic Team

Setting a Framework

Once the student's needs are identified, it is time to establish a potential framework to support the student and determine what the perfect academic team might look like. For instance, you might realize that the student needs subject support in English and biology (from subject experts), some minor assistance from a motivator, and a strong discipline coach. So, ideally, you might already have a good idea of who and what to look for.

Depending on how much support the student needs in each sphere, the importance of each role can be determined. It's also important to prioritize ruthlessly. What's the greatest area in which the student needs support? For instance, let's say that a student's confidence has just hit an all-time low and his motivation level has also taken a huge dive. In this case, the motivator should be placed as the primary professional required for this particular student's academic team. Then, secondary needs will determine the other pieces of the puzzle that might be required.

At this point, don't be concerned with how many professionals will be required (especially since some professionals may take more than one role) or who these people may be—just focus on what will be required in order to support the student and enable him or her to succeed.

Evaluating Professionals

At this point, it's time to look at whoever is already in place and evaluate their roles, especially in view of the recently designed framework, which is what the ideal academic team would need. This evaluation should include any independent professionals in place, as well as school professionals who may have a good degree of influence on the student.

For instance, perhaps a student has a great football coach who he finds very inspiring, so this person may already be playing the role of a motivator. Now, it will be important to evaluate and understand the limitations of the relationship between the coach and the student. In this particular example, it could be that the student is unable to transfer his level of confidence and motivation from sports to the academic sphere. So in this way, the coach is limited in the role of a motivator, since the student will also need someone to inspire and motivate him to achieve greatness in academics.

Now, the importance of evaluating these already established relationships also lies in considering what does and doesn't work, taking into account factors such as personality match-ups and frequency of meetings.

Also, evaluate existing tutors to see if they already play additional roles aside from that of a subject expert. In this case, such a role could be recognized and valued. For example, if a biology tutor helps a student to get very well organized, perhaps he or she can dedicate some extra time to focus exclusively on those skills, aside from the tutoring sessions (thereby also performing the role of a discipline coach or planner).

Reaching Out

After you have evaluated the professionals who are currently working with the student, it is time to reach out and start looking for the support that isn't already in place (while bearing in mind the framework that was already considered). Of course, this may be the hardest part of the process. But with the tips and strategies we go through in this book, the whole experience should be easier (and you should be able to save both time and money while finding great professionals).

At this point, it is important to be open-minded. As I have already mentioned before, too many parents are victims of having overly narrow expectations, simply rejecting the idea of working

Chapter 2: The Academic Team

with specific professionals who don't meet certain requirements when they would, in reality, be great additions to the academic team if they were actually hired.

Now, how can you determine if your requirements and expectations are indeed too narrow and may be preventing you from finding great talent for the academic team? This goes back to getting to the heart of the student's needs. Once they are determined, what should and shouldn't be a requirement will become clearer. Let's say you are looking for a biology tutor since your child is struggling with the subject in their junior year of high school. As long as the person has a great understanding of the subject at that level and is able to teach it well to your child, does it really matter if he or she has a PhD in biology? Note that I am using this as an example, since it is a common "requirement" for parents to expect an incredibly high level of education to tutor their children at various levels.

That being said, also be careful with the other end of the spectrum; parents also need to be patient. Some, in desperation, will hire anyone who loosely falls into the general vicinity of who and what they are looking for. However, this mistake may be a bit easier to fix than the previous one. Why is that? Well, if you realize that the professional doesn't actually meet your expectations, you can simply let him or her go.

Managing

Once everything is in place, it is easy for parents to just "forget" about it. As I will discuss a bit further under "Frequency of Communication & Using Mini-Reports," parents should look for a happy medium between checking in too frequently and completely ignoring everything for long stretches of time (or doing so until a crisis pops out of nowhere). It is important to evaluate the student's progress while communicating periodically with team members for feedback. When red flags arise, it may be necessary to step in.

Additionally, there can also be times when the student questions the impact of individual members of the academic team and times when the student's confidence wavers. If that happens and you actually have a strong team in place, do your best to consider things objectively and carefully before giving up on any specific professional. As "team manager," the parent will often have to follow his or her instincts when making such decisions.

In an analogous fashion, how many times in professional sports have we seen a dismal season played by a team, causing the fans to almost beg the general manager to trade key players in it? However, by maintaining those key players that disappointed their fans in a previous season, the team may go on to win the championship. Similarly, parents often need to be patient when waiting for results. Patience in this regard usually pays off, and in leading an academic team, as long as the right people are in it, the story is no different.

Managing for Extremely Busy Parents

Now, what if you are the kind of parent who is just so busy that you have very little time to actually manage the academic team once it is in place?

If that is your case, you could then hire an "academic team manager." It doesn't have to be as expensive as it sounds, since parents could pay someone on an hourly basis—about one or two hours every two or three weeks—in order to check in with team members and monitor the student's progress. The professional's required background will depend entirely on what will ultimately be required of him or her. In most cases, if all the professional needs to do is speak with the team members on a regular basis and watch out for red flags, someone reliable with experience as a personal or executive assistant would most likely be able to do a satisfactory job.

Paying for the Academic Team on a Budget

As we mentioned before, many parents may be thinking that having and managing an academic team may be an extremely expensive venture. However, it definitely does not have to be. If parents are patient and put effort into managing the academic team, they may be able to spend very little money and still provide their children with the support needed to enable them to reach their potential. Now, how would that work (in addition to employing the strategies mentioned under "Finding a Good Tutor on a Budget")?

Many roles in the academic team could essentially be provided by professionals who would be willing to do so on a pro-bono basis in a mentorship-type arrangement. The challenge would be to find these willing professionals, work around their schedule, and get the students deeply committed and on board with the system.

Another option that could be completely free would be to get family members and friends to assist in supporting the student, as long as they have enough expertise. The challenge will, of course, be finding good matches in this case. However, for parents with extensive professional (and personal) networks, it might not be that challenging to find people who would be able to fill most of, if not all, of the roles required for an excellent academic team.

As previously discussed, it may essentially be quicker and easier to assemble a high quality team when one is willing and able to spend money on the best professionals available. However, it is entirely possible to put together a fantastic team while on a budget, especially when investing a bit more time and effort into the search for the right professionals.

How Much Input Should the Student Have Regarding the Team?

When it comes to making any decisions about the academic team, how much input and control should the student have? None? Some? Or total?

That is a difficult question to answer, because it will definitely depend on the student's personality, maturity level and self-awareness. Ideally, regardless of these factors, parents and students should always agree on the decisions made. When that becomes challenging, it is important to remind all parties that

Chapter 2: The Academic Team

everyone essentially has the same goal: for the student to be successful.

Needless to say, if the student is highly independent, it is usually a good idea to give him or her the freedom to make decisions regarding the academic team more directly. In case a particular decision made by the student doesn't yield a good outcome, the student can take it as a learning experience, hopefully either accepting more input in the future or avoiding past mistakes to make better decisions in the long run.

For instance, Connor was a student who was very confident in dealing with issues on his own. His parents had tried to convince him to get a math tutor when his grades started to dip at the beginning of his junior year, but he was very reluctant to accept any help. After a few months he realized that he should have accepted the help, since his grades started to go down even further, and he soon concluded that his decision to reject the help had been a bit naive. This is, of course, a simple and straightforward example of how this kind of situation usually unfolds, and it may sound very familiar to a lot of parents. Now, with the strategies we have already discussed (for getting students on board), cases such as this one can usually be avoided.

Communicating with the Team

Communicating Expectations

It is absolutely crucial for parents and team members to share their expectations regarding the professional relationship. Every element should be discussed—from punctuality to the expected academic results of the student(s). By doing so, everyone is on the same page and issues can be avoided. Frank conversations at the beginning of the professional relationship can save parents, professionals, and students from a lot of grief in the long run.

Parents should communicate their expectations regarding the student's academic results and a potential timeline for them, in order to make sure they are in line with those of the educational professionals. Naturally, since parents are investing time and (very often) money into the relationship with the academic team, many have the tendency to expect quick and very positive results. The educational professionals, on the other hand, will be more likely to have a better idea of what can be expected, given their experience with other students. As a result, bringing the two into reconciliation is very important.

Also, when parents have specific expectations about how the work should be performed, it is important to share them with the academic team. For instance, if the professional is a tutor, is he or she expected to give the student homework? Is the tutor expected to write small reports to the parents every once in a while? All these expectations should be laid on the table from the outset.

Finally, don't forget to work out small details regarding the professional's relationship (especially if the professional works independently). For example, who is in charge of setting up and cancelling sessions, the parents or the students? Who determines the frequency of sessions? Should the professional's performance be reviewed, and if so, how often? Having clear answers to these questions can prevent a lot of unnecessary headaches.

Requesting Utmost Honesty

Almost needless to say, it is critical for parents to ask academic team members for openness and complete honesty—especially when there are indications that the student may need more support. Whenever there are signs that a crisis may be around the corner, it is preferable that the professional lets the student's parents know right away so that they can take appropriate measures, if and when required.

Most students have the tendency to underestimate the scope of any crisis at school, and many also have the tendency to overestimate their ability to quickly recover from dire academic situations. What that often leads to is having students bringing home report cards that are below parents' expectations, often when no warning signs had popped up before. Consequently, it should be a duty of the academic team to assist parents in understanding where the student is standing (occasionally if things are going well) while keeping them informed in case any sort of bad sign, indicative of an issue, appears on the horizon.

Therefore, it is of great importance for parents to require utmost honesty from all members of the academic team in order to ensure good performance and prevent potential issues that could otherwise be avoided.

Frequency of Communication & Using Mini-Reports

Now, how often should a parent communicate with the team professionals? If you have a team manager, he or she can do the job for you. For new professionals, check in after the first couple of sessions to get some input, then request a mini-report about every few weeks (exceptions would

Chapter 2: The Academic Team

include team members who meet with the students less frequently than once a month). Unless there's a red flag somewhere, there is no major need to communicate more frequently.

What should the mini-report include? Observations on student motivation, level of preparation and general remarks on how to keep things improving. Optimally, it should be something that you are willing to read—something quick and to the point. Note that some overly-excited professionals may be happy to spend a lot of time writing up impressive reports that might be as long as a serious academic essay. However, that usually isn't necessary, except for unusual cases that might need special attention.

In order to simplify things even further, the mini-report could simply grade the student's level (student motivation, level of preparation, engagement, etc.) on a scale from 1 to 10, perhaps with one or two sentences explaining the situation when necessary. Whenever the levels are too low, a parent should dig a bit deeper.

Please note: Beware of false alarms, and avoid overly high expectations and overreactions. These often lead to wasting one's time, energy and resources. Imagine, for instance, a parent who expects the professional's report to show a 9 or higher on both motivation and engagement every two weeks. However, the professional simply reports a 6 or a 7 out of 10 for the student's engagement level. Because of this, the parent makes a big fuss—calling in a meeting with the professional, nagging the student, etc... Such actions would likely only frustrate the student while, if done frequently, erode the level of trust in the relationship with the professional. Not to mention it would mount added pressure onto the student and potentially hinder the dynamic between the professional and the student, which wouldn't lead to anything positive. Many parents' overreactions simply contribute to the detriment of the situation.

To be quite honest, some parents do have a tendency to overreact to a certain extent when the situation doesn't look as promising as expected. That is perfectly understandable, since they want to do whatever they can to help their children succeed. However, it is important to take a step back in case an overreaction takes away from the effectiveness of a plan that is already in place.

There are also parents on the other end of the spectrum, especially those who are overly busy, with the tendency to ignore red flags and warning signs; hoping that everything will sort itself out on its own.

Chapter 2: The Academic Team

However, unfortunately, that often won't be the case.

To avoid both ends of the spectrum, my suggestion would be the following: After a couple of reports with lower scores than expected, just ask the professional (or professionals) directly involved what he or she thinks would help the situation in order to boost each score. That will usually be enough in determining what steps to take next.

About every month or so, even when there aren't warning signs, be sure to have a chat with the professionals, including the team manager (if you have one), and the student. A short one will usually suffice. Beware the tendency of both students and certain professionals to say, "Everything is just fine," and dig just a bit deeper every now and then. For independent-minded students, you can say something along the lines of "How are you feeling about the subject(s) and the professional(s)? I don't want to bug you all the time about it but just give me a heads up if you think it would be good for me to step in."

Also, in case you request for the professional to give you lots of recurring feedback, offer to pay them for their time accordingly. Some parents feel that if they are paying any professional any amount of money, then they are entitled to frequent "customer service". If you do expect frequent communication with the professional beyond the regular paid time, and feel that it should be included in the regular hourly fee, clarify that with the person in advance.

Asking for Updates in Front of the Student

Something I have always found interesting is how often parents would ask, "How did it go?" directly after a tutoring session...right in front of the student! Needless to say, I would always try to be as diplomatic as possible in my response.

Now, imagine that a specific tutoring session was very unproductive. After the session, one of the student's parents asks the professional how things went. Even if the session was completely unproductive due to the student's poor attention level (or something along those lines), it would be rather tactless of the professional to criticize the student to his parent(s) with him or her being present. It would certainly be much better for the academic team member to say something like, "Well, we've got some work ahead of us," and communicate with the parent afterwards. From the parents' perspective, it may be better not to put the professional on the spot and simply contact them later to check in.

Chapter 2: The Academic Team

The Team's Relationship with the School Staff

Ideally, the team communicates often with the school staff, including teachers and counselors. Naturally, we need to be understanding when teachers are really busy and aren't able to communicate frequently. Especially during exam season, it is normal for teachers to get overwhelmed with questions from students' parents, guardians, and tutors. Whenever the student is struggling with a particular subject, it's a great idea to get in touch with the teacher to understand how the student can make a recovery (at least from the teacher's point of view). However, it is optimal not to wait for that to happen and to build a relationship with teachers—especially teachers of subjects that the students have struggled with before.

Note: Whenever the student isn't getting the grades he or she hoped for (or expected), it's often tempting to perceive the teacher as the villain. Of course, not all teachers are perfect, but it's important to at least put a genuine and conscious effort into understanding why the student isn't performing as expected before making assumptions about the professional.

CHAPTER 3: COMMON ISSUES—STRATEGIES AND TIPS

The Student Hits a Plateau— Complacency Sets In

Let me present a very common story. A student starts working with a specific professional and things start going very well. Motivation and confidence levels skyrocket, and there is excitement regarding what could be accomplished. The first few quizzes, exams and projects show improvement and everyone is happy. The professional is happy because his methods are working; the student is happy because it now seems like he or she has the potential to succeed; and the parents are happy because it looks like their investment in hiring the professional is actually paying off! However, after a certain amount of time, perhaps a few months, progress stalls. Or, even worse, the student's grades take a bit of a nosedive.

But how could that be? What happened to the heroic professional? Has he gotten comfortable and started putting less effort into helping the student, consequently leading to poor results? Has he become complacent? No, not necessarily (although that could be the case, of course).

Usually, we can attribute most plateaus to the comfort and familiarity that develops in the

Chapter 3: Common Issues—Strategies and Tips

relationship between the student and the professional(s). Quite simply, the initial positive change, which was triggered by the introduction of new and exciting methods brought forth by the professional, slowly gets replaced by the student's old habits which slowly creep back into the scene.

Imagine, for instance, that Bob is struggling in math and his family hires a tutor, Eric. Once they start working together, Bob gets excited about math again, because Eric is able to explain things very clearly. As a result, Bob's confidence level in math rises, which triggers him to do more homework and practice math exercises more often. That, in turn, leads him to see an increase in his success. Better quiz and test grades reinforce the idea that things are going well. With regular tutoring sessions, however, Bob slowly starts to take his foot off the accelerator... Bob thinks that Eric's method is infallible and that as long as he is getting tutored by Eric, his grades in math will continue to rise. Slowly, complacency sets in and Bob's old habits come back. He no longer practices as often as he did when they started with the tutoring sessions. As a result, his grades go back down.

So, in this case, who's to blame? It's easy to point the finger and say that Bob's guilty! After all, he was the one who took his foot off the accelerator.

However, he was actually convinced that, after his initial boost in confidence, he had reached a good enough level in math from which he wouldn't decline. As much as this reasoning may sound naive, it is adopted often, since it is quite common for students to overestimate their level of skill in a specific subject—and they can't usually be blamed for that, since they don't usually have the tools to evaluate their own skill set.

Looking at this situation from that angle, Eric, the tutor, may be a bit more to blame than Bob. How so? Because Eric, as an educator, could have evaluated Bob's skill set on a more regular basis. Had he done that, he would have realized that Bob needed to step it up a notch once he started becoming more complacent and he could have consequently let Bob know. However, Eric's blame is not necessarily that big either. After all, Bob was acting very confident about math, so Bob's confidence may have signalled to Eric that everything was in order and that Bob was practicing math very regularly.

Of course, each case should be carefully analyzed on an individual basis. That being said, all too often, both parties (professional and student) are somewhat guilty thereof, yet neither ill-intended. However, the good news is that we can take steps to actually prevent complacency from creeping into the scene. So let's take a step back to discuss what can be done in order to help students steer clear from a false sense of security.

How to Avoid Complacency Altogether

Avoiding complacency comes down to two things: the frequency (and quality) of monitoring the student's progress and excellent communication. Note that the professionals' mini-reports, as we suggested under "Frequency of Communication & Using Mini-Reports," should be enough to maintain a healthy frequency of communication between parents and professionals. However, we also want to explore the monitoring and reporting in more detail, especially with regard to how it can prevent complacency.

When it comes to the frequency of monitoring students' progress, as we have already hinted at before, more doesn't mean better; especially when it comes to parents asking students directly. Naturally, the academic team members should also be doing a good portion of the monitoring, since they often are in a better position to do so.

Chapter 3: Common Issues—Strategies and Tips

One must find the optimal frequency of monitoring, carefully considering each set of unique circumstances, especially bearing in mind the way each specific student communicates with his/her parent(s) and with academic team member(s). If a parent or the professional monitors too frequently, the student may get frustrated. If a parent or the professional doesn't monitor frequently enough, things could potentially get derailed. As a result, it is important to find the happy medium.

What about the quality of monitoring? Now, let's focus primarily on the monitoring done by the parents. Each parent may have a different idea of how they may optimally monitor the student's progress. One critical consideration is what exactly should be monitored? Just performance in terms of grades? Surely not, since there are several underlying factors that will affect students' grades—and these factors will often be a much better measure of student progress, not to mention the fact that school grades are often not fully within a student's scope of control. For instance, what if a teacher gives his or her class a pop quiz in a concept that the student hasn't covered yet due to a sports trip? A bad grade, on this occasion, would be no great reflection of the student's commitment or dedication.

Chapter 3: Common Issues—Strategies and Tips

So what are the factors that can better measure student performance? Motivation and engagement levels are significant ones (as suggested for the mini-reports). The only challenge, however, lies in accurately measuring such factors due to their qualitative nature. So why are these better progress measures than grades? First of all, report cards don't come often and it usually becomes cumbersome to keep track of every single quiz, and dig out a lot of meaning from each and every variation of a student's grades. For instance, if a student gets 86% in one quiz and 78% in the following quiz, it could just mean that the second quiz was harder than the first. One cannot and should not squeeze out much significance from small variations in results. Naturally, not a lot of meaning should be extracted from small variations in motivation and engagement levels either—but these two factors certainly deserve a great deal of attention. Without enough of them, the student simply won't perform nearly as well as he or she could.

So how can we effectively monitor both motivation and engagement? Of course, one must have an open level of communication with the team professionals (as discussed before), so that they can inform the parent in case motivation and engagement go too far below the expected mark.

Chapter 3: Common Issues—Strategies and Tips

Naturally, whenever specific levels dip too far below the average, it is probably time to step in. However, it is important to consider a few things before doing so.

When & How to "Step In"

According to most students, parents simply step in too often. Based on my long experience communicating with parents and students, I strongly recommend that parents and professionals try to develop a habit of offering the student support before actually diving into an issue and volunteering raw opinions.

Let's say Bob comes back home and shows his mother a bad report card. She thinks she knows why he didn't perform that well. Instead of showing immediate despair, pity or even disappointment, I would argue that nine times out of ten, parents would be better off just letting the student know they have confidence in his or her skills of handling the situation on their own, but they will be there in case they can help in any way.

I can already imagine mothers saying, "But I am the mother and I have tremendous insight into my child's needs and also on how they can improve at school! It sounds like you are suggesting I now have

Chapter 3: Common Issues—Strategies and Tips

to ask for permission to share my thoughts with my own son or daughter!"

If a mother were to tell me this, I would say that it is a great thing that she has tremendous insight into her child's needs, but chances are the student from our example, Bob, would be more open and would feel less smothered if his mother would (at least initially) show confidence in his ability to handle the situation on his own, and then offer to help.

That being said, once a parent determines that he or she should step in given a specific situation, it becomes a matter of determining how much attention and effort each case requires—keeping in mind there is an arsenal of tools, as we outline throughout this book, at his or her disposal.

As I mentioned before, some parents may have a tendency to overreact when they decide to step in. My suggestion is for parents to dig around a bit before making any quick decisions. Ask the educational professionals for their opinions, especially the ones who work most often with the student (the members of the academic team as well as teachers and counselors at school), to inquire about what may be most beneficial given the situation. That in itself might reveal the most optimal approach moving forward.

Chapter 3: Common Issues—Strategies and Tips

As another example, Francine comes home with a terrible report card, including lower-than-expected grades in a subject that she is getting tutored in. Her mother may feel quite frustrated that the tutoring she paid for with her hard-earned money hasn't translated into concrete results. Additionally, she might feel that Francine just isn't putting in the effort, and that she needs quite a bit of nagging to improve. Also, the teacher at school seems really unfair. So Francine's mother's first impulse is to "roast" the tutor, ground her daughter for slacking off, request a parent-teacher interview and leave twenty furious messages on the answering machine in case she can't get one scheduled fast enough. But of course, after thinking things through, she decides to email the tutor and the teacher to find out where things went wrong and in what area her daughter can improve. She might, for instance, find out that Francine is under a lot of pressure and stress due to extra-curricular activities; or she might find out that the rest of the class did actually worse than her daughter. She usually won't find out until she digs a bit deeper, and often initial assumptions may just crumble down after a couple of emails or phone calls.

So I would say: take a step back, communicate with the team, and do your best to avoid nagging before getting some good insights on the whole situation. But what if the situation seems to be a bit worse than originally thought?

Dealing with an Academic Crisis

When the Student's Results Are Lower than Expected

So, let's say that everything seemed just fine, then suddenly the student appears to hit a sequence of adverse events—for instance, a series of terrible exam grades. One of the most important things, just as we suggested in the previous section, is for parents to try to be as objective as possible and avoid making any rash decisions before gathering enough information from all sources. Additionally, it is fundamental for the professional who plays the role of the motivator to give the student a lot of support so that he or she can turn things around. Finally, it's essential to find the source of the problem before taking action.

Often in this type of situation, just as we mentioned under "The Student Hits a Plateau—Complacency Sets In," all parties involved are somewhat innocent. For instance, perhaps nobody had much of a clue that the student wasn't well prepared for a specific exam, and then events started to snowball as a result, leading to the "crisis".

However, what if there is actually someone to blame? Let's start with the possibility that there is actually a "villain". Moreover, let's get started by analyzing what should unfold, in case one of the professionals (a tutor, for instance) is the one to blame for the situation.

What If the Professional from the Academic Team Is to Blame?

So, if the "villain" is the professional, to what extent is he or she guilty? And what was he or she guilty of? Many parents feel somewhat awkward about questioning the performance of the professional, since that may seem like a somewhat aggressive or impolite thing to do. However, it's the parents' right to try and understand what is happening. After all, it's the parents' investment at stake. It's often their money, their time, and their children's education we are talking about. That being said, of course it's better to be tactful and avoid implying anything before actual facts come to the surface.

Has the professional been negligent or just complacent? Did he or she have access to enough information to know something negative (a bad test result, poor grade on the report card, etc.) was about to happen? If not, did he have the means to evaluate the student's performance prior to the negative event? If so, why didn't he or she take action? Can anything be learned by this situation so similar cases can be avoided in the future?

One consideration: sometimes, it is indeed very challenging for a professional to understand the teacher's expectations or to truly comprehend the standards of a specific exam on the horizon. However, if the result is well below expectations, it may be the case that he or she is actually not a good match for the student. The key is to gain understanding of what has contributed to the failure.

Was it due to lack of skill? In that case, the solution is, of course, an obvious one: just find a more skilled professional. Was he or she just lazy or negligent? In that case, perhaps, the parent should also ask for a refund. Next, he or she should go back to our system in order to potentially hire a new professional (or professionals, if necessary).

On the other hand, if the parent decides in favor of keeping the professional(s) employed after all, it becomes important to put a strategy in place, together, to avoid similar situations in the future. One thing to keep in mind that is worth mentioning here: don't always just assume the professional is doing a terrific job. Throughout the years, I have seen many parents remain too lenient in view of situations in which they should have taken action. In order to avoid that, always remember to try your best to be as objective as possible, and take action accordingly if the situation demands it.

Of course the professional won't always be the one to blame. Sometimes, you may find that he or she was doing a good job and either the student and perhaps the teacher (or more often the dynamic between the two) may be more to blame.

What If the Student Is to Blame?

Often, busy students start neglecting a course, thinking rather innocently that everything is under control until they actually hit a huge road bump. The mounting pressure, busy schedules and an intensely competitive environment are often more to blame than the students themselves.

Frequently, parents put too much blame on the students before taking a broad view of the situation. That may only further pressure and frustrate the student; the results thereof usually being unpredictable and, more often than not, quite negative. In this type of situation, often times, the student was simply not aware of the level of dedication that a specific topic or subject required.

Another consideration: Quite commonly, the student's busy schedule of sports and other activities interferes too much with the school. Sometimes, a certain degree of sacrifice is required in balancing academics and extra activities. Is the student always exhausted after certain activities? That may be a sign that more time should be allocated to academics instead.

Don't get me wrong—I strongly believe sports and additional activities are remarkably important. However, it's critical to find a healthy balance between them and a student's academics. More can be found on this topic under "Balancing Sports and Academics."

Student-Teacher Dynamic

What If the Student Has a Bad Relationship with the Teacher?

From experience, the greatest source of disagreements between teachers and students is how the teacher perceives the student's level of effort in his or her class. Sometimes it doesn't take much for a student to make a bad impression on the teacher, especially when the teacher is on the strict side. Consequently, over 80% of the time, a student and teacher relationship can be improved (re-established or restored) once the student tries hard to demonstrate genuine effort and interest.

Moreover, once teachers see that there is a dedicated system in place to assist a student who is genuinely interested in succeeding (while putting good effort into it), they often change their opinions (in case they were negative beforehand), and also start to root for the student. If the student demonstrates great effort and he or she still doesn't get along with the teacher, the key is <u>extra</u> dedication. What's not to like about a student who steps up to the plate and gives 100% in a class? If a student brings his or her "A" game to class every day and puts great effort into mastering the subject, anyone who isn't rooting for the student is just going to end up looking foolish!

Of course, there will still be teachers who the student will simply be unable to get along with, no matter how hard the student tries. In this case, it is important that the pupil tries his or her best to stay focused and work hard on the class, regardless of anything else. If the student is willing to rebuild the relationship with the teacher and takes steps to do so, all the better. If not, it is important to try to get the student to commit to "minimize the damage," to work really hard, and not let the situation affect the way he or she enjoys the subject (or the course).

Chapter 3: Common Issues—Strategies and Tips

How many times have you heard someone say to you, "I used to be good at (insert a specific subject here) until I had this one teacher... He (or she) was so (insert unsavoury adjective here) that I just started hating the subject and didn't do well in it ever again!" As an educator, I can say with confidence that I have heard these words (or variations thereof) way too many times, and that's a sad thing! I wouldn't know how often the teachers were actually to blame—perhaps many of the students could have put in an extra effort to patch things up and overcome the issue in order to succeed in the subject, but that is beside the point. The really sad thing is that, regardless of who is blame, these students started to dislike a specific subject because of the situation, and usually that led them to underperform as students in that topic.

The academic team can play a crucial role in this type of situation in order to prevent the student from taking an intense dislike to a particular subject or area of study. A great tutor, for instance, could uplift the student's spirits and help him or her perform well, regardless of the student's relationship with the teacher.

Overdependence on the Academic Team

How to Avoid the Pitfalls Thereof

Many students often develop a strong bond with specific members of the academic team, especially when they are doing a great job together. For example, a student could develop a great relationship with her tutor and may feel like she couldn't perform as well in the long run without the tutor's help. For many students, even a small level of dependence can eventually reach higher levels, and their confidence in specific subjects can take a dive when the professional isn't around. So how can one avoid this type of situation?

It is fundamental to manage the students' expectations when getting help from the academic team. Essentially, the student shouldn't fall into the trap of becoming dependent on the professional's help from a psychological standpoint. This can be avoided with open conversations involving the student and the team members. I recall one my students who had a great relationship with a tutor and his father would always tease him and say, "Hey Jimmy, remember Mr. James won't be taking your college exams next year!"—a little reminder for

Chapter 3: Common Issues—Strategies and Tips

Jimmy not to become too psychologically dependent on Mr. James' tutoring.

Additionally, it is important for the academic team to keep the full development of students as its primary goal. That is, the team ought to focus on completely empowering students and giving them the tools to thrive on their own. It is paramount that the professionals display a commitment towards teaching the student concepts, methods, and strategies that they can use in the long run. It is important to note that it becomes tempting to overlook these things when there are pressing, immediate needs at hand.

For instance, if the student has an important exam on the horizon, it is likely that both the student and the professional (let's assume a tutor in this case) will be primarily focused on the task at hand while "forgetting" to focus on covering lasting study skills, which the student can benefit from in the long run. Then once that exam is done, perhaps there will be another quiz coming up, so the student and the tutor focus exclusively on preparing for that; thereafter there will be another test coming up and so on and so forth, leaving little time and space to focus on the fundamental learning and study skills that will stick with the student and empower him or her throughout his or her entire academic career.

Therefore, it becomes important to remind the professional at least every once in a while that these skills should be focused on in order to empower the student, not to mention how such strategies and methods ought to be implemented throughout the course of the sessions between students and professionals.

CHAPTER 4: STUDENTS—APPROACHING THEIR UNIQUENESS

What (Academic) Level is the Student Currently At?

Personally, I find it rather useless to put a permanent label on any student. That's why, instead of defining "types" of students, I will create three levels that we can use to define any specific student's current situation. Note (as you are probably already well aware of) that students can often change levels rather suddenly and unexpectedly at times, while in other cases, students may change levels slowly and progressively.

Depending on the student's current level, the academic team should take different roles and shapes, focusing on specific areas of concern. For instance, a student who is already getting very high grades will usually need a lot less motivation, compared to a student who is failing a few subjects. Hence, the role of motivator won't be as crucial in this student's academic team. This may be obvious to some parents, but the topic should still be explored in detail to optimize results and to help students reach their full potential.

Let's define the three levels as follows:

- Level A: students getting straight As

Chapter 4: Students—Approaching Their Uniqueness

- Level B: students getting Bs and C+s

- Level C: students getting Cs and below

Level "A" Students

Level "A" students only need enough support to remain at a high level and potentially bring their marks as close to 100% as possible. They are often highly motivated, so their academic team doesn't need to necessarily place tremendous focus on motivation. Instead, they need a high level academic support for specific subjects in order for their grades to remain at a high level and not to let them slip.

Many level "A" students are, surprisingly, somewhat disorganized. In that case, the support of a discipline coach can be very helpful.

Another common challenge for level "A" students is overconfidence and a bit of complacency after enjoying a lot of success. Once students are getting straight As and "relax" a bit, focusing more time and energy on extra-curricular activities and social life, the grades can suddenly take unexpected dips. Every now and then, it is tempting for these high achievers to take their foot off the accelerator, especially when the work ethic of their friends isn't as impressive. So, when that happens and the grades do slip, what should be done?

Chapter 4: Students—Approaching Their Uniqueness

The good news is, it doesn't often take too much for such students to bounce back, focus and recover. However, when the slip is significant, the strategies we suggest for level "B" and "C" students should be implemented.

According to many parents of high achieving students, it is important to show support without "freaking out" too much when slips do occur. It is also worthwhile to note that, according to many students, a lot of parents have the tendency to smother them with support during a crisis. As discussed in further detail under "How to Step In," it is worthwhile to mention that students who have very independent personalities will often respond more positively to their parents offering support without initially jumping in with too much involvement.

Level "B" Students

Students that often get Bs and C+s are often "stuck" at this level for long periods of time. Very often, they have what it takes to step up without tremendous effort, but they may not see the benefit and the payoff of putting a lot more energy and time into studying, since the improvement in grades usually comes at progressively higher levels of effort. For instance, for a student to go from a C+ to a B, it

Chapter 4: Students—Approaching Their Uniqueness

might take an extra three or four hours of studying a week, while it may take him or her an extra ten or fifteen hours a week to get from a B to an A.

Psychologically speaking, students that appear to be stuck in this level have, in a way, simply settled—especially when they are only struggling with one or two subjects. It becomes a matter of their personal standards, and even very confident students may justify the situation by thinking something along the lines of, "Well, I usually get C+s and Bs in math but I am very successful in sports and I usually do much better in English and biology, so performing like that in math is no big deal!"

So how can parents and educators raise the students' standards? Someone playing the role of motivator in the academic team will be of great importance in this scenario. The professional, if influential, can have a strong positive effect on the student's standards. For instance, if a tutor plays the role of a motivator, he or she can simply say, "You know what, you can get an A. It might seem like a steep ladder but through hard work, we can make it happen."

That being said, the person doesn't even really need to be an integral part of the academic team. Anyone who could potentially light the fire and inspire the student can help. A student's mother

Chapter 4: Students—Approaching Their Uniqueness

once told me she brought an impressive friend over for dinner—he was both a doctor and a lawyer. Not only that, he was also an impressive athlete on the side (a marathon runner). That dinner alone was enough for the student to raise his standards and step it up a notch in school. The student told me afterwards that he had thought, "Well, if Dr. Smith can be both a doctor and a lawyer, why can't I achieve great things and do great in school?" Note that the student wasn't even interested in law or medicine as career paths, but the doctor's level of success was enough to inspire him.

Naturally, there are cases in which such an event could have the opposite effect: the student could feel intimidated and think he or she is way beneath the impressive person's level. If that is a remote possibility, a few positive words from the person are often enough to avoid any negative outcomes. Something like, "You know what, I can tell you have the potential to make things happen." That's it. But of course, it has to be very sincere; otherwise the student might just think the person is being a phony. These days, most youth can sense and detect dishonesty (especially when coming from adults) right away.

Chapter 4: Students—Approaching Their Uniqueness

Level "C" Students

When students repeatedly underperform and get grades below C+s, they need a great boost in motivation. However, they are also the toughest ones to convince that they can indeed turn things around. For that, it is crucial to bring their confidence back up to a reasonable level. Once the initial inertia is overcome and they can see that there is hope, it usually isn't that hard for them to climb up to "level B."

Let's talk about the psychological inertia that is usually present in the mind of a student at this level. We can start with an exaggerated example of a student who is doing poorly in most or all subjects. He used to do much better a few years prior, but things started sliding downhill for various reasons. At this point, he feels he is terrible at school and that's just the way things are. With a self-defeating mindset, it becomes a self-fulfilling prophecy every time he gets a bad grade. He feels that effort won't translate into higher grades, which is completely untrue, unbeknownst to him.

So the key is to get this student to put effort into studying hard, just so he gets that first good quiz or exam grade in order for him to realize that he can actually do well if he applies himself. There must be hope and there must be someone who demonstrates

Chapter 4: Students—Approaching Their Uniqueness

a great deal of belief in the student at this point. However, chances are that hope will only re-appear after an initial effort followed by a victory, no matter how small it might be. The student must be convinced that hard work will pay off, and that is a tough sell before he actually experiences it and "sees it with his own eyes." Words alone won't necessarily do the trick when the situation is dire.

Imagine a sports team that has lost the previous ten straight games. In the locker room, the players probably don't even have the heart to look each other in the face after every game. It seems almost inevitable that the trend will continue and that they will keep losing games, unless something changes. The key might be in having the coach deliver one of those awe-inspiring speeches to turn things around, telling the players to give their all in the next game. It can all change after just one victory, which could then shift each player's mindset.

The most important thing is to believe (and remember) is that there is always hope. As an educator, I have seen a great deal of students improve from absolutely dismal grades to achieving levels they never thought were possible for them. With the right academic team in place, students can turn things around and recover as long as they persevere and stay the course.

Chapter 4: Students—Approaching Their Uniqueness

Students with Learning Disabilities

Nowadays, a great number of students are diagnosed with learning disabilities. The sad thing is, many of them simply feel like they are at a natural disadvantage when competing with other students in academics. For that reason, it is important to offer them enough support so they can feel confident and have a solid chance to prove to themselves that they can perform just as well, if not better, than other students.

Throughout my career as an educator, I have worked with several students that had been diagnosed with learning disabilities, and many of them have had great success in academics—graduating from great programs and renowned colleges.

Of course, it is important for parents to hire professionals who are well qualified to deal with the student's specific learning disability when applicable. Certain disabilities are best dealt with by professionals who have been trained in very specific programs, so it is important for parents to do some research before hiring educational professionals to work with their children and make sure that the professionals are qualified to help.

Additionally, I believe the key is for students to do their absolute best to learn how a disability might restrict them, and find effective ways to work around these conditions. That way, they can feel that their learning disability won't hold them back in their quest to follow their dreams.

As an example of success, Barbara, a dyslexic student working with the assistance of great professionals and supporting parents, was able to graduate from a highly renowned business program after being able to impressively thrive in challenging courses throughout her academic career. After graduation, she was able to get an excellent job at a marketing firm and pursue an extremely successful career, despite the challenges associated with her dyslexia.

Students with Very Busy Schedules

Balancing Sports and Academics

Nowadays, it seems like a great deal of students commit to a large number of other activities, especially sports, which might get in the way of their studying. I have come across students that were in four or more sports teams during the course of their academic year. However fantastic and impressive that might be, it is undeniable that the sports schedule would often significantly interfere with the students' academic performance. So the big question is: how can you find the right balance and where should the line be drawn where a student may be better off quitting a sports team or a specific physical activity, in order to have more time to focus on academics?

I should definitely stress that my views on sports for students are actually quite positive. I am very confident that sports have a significantly positive impact on the lives of students on many different levels. I would even go as far as suggesting that every single student should actively engage in at least one regular sports activity (unless some condition denies him or her the possibility thereof), given the positive psychological, social, and physical effects associated with it.

Getting that thought out of the way, for students with an incredibly busy sports schedule, I would recommend that they try to genuinely answer the following questions: "Does my commitment to sports have a negative effect on my grades at school? And if so, to what extent?" If the answer to the first question is "yes," and the answer to the second question is "significant" (or anything along those lines), I would strongly suggest that the student take a good step back to re-evaluate their priorities and

Chapter 4: Students—Approaching Their Uniqueness

act accordingly. The real issue here is that the answers to these questions aren't always clear and many students are often in denial, unwilling to admit that sports are having a negative effect on their grades.

I can already imagine some parents saying, "But academics aren't everything! My children are great at sports and that is a big part of who they are. They can't just quit because their grades at school are below expectations. They just need to study harder, get tutored, work hard, and keep going with sports!"

If that is what you are thinking, even if to a lesser extent, I would say I strongly respect that attitude. But just like adults, young people can also burn out. Sometimes, the point at which that will happen is not very clear. I have personally met a great deal of students who were real warriors. They would just never quit, no matter how stressed, overburdened or burned out they were. While their attitude was remarkable, not to mention their commitment, sometimes I just wondered if they ever took a break to think about their priorities, even if just for a second. I believe these students can often truly benefit from stepping aside for a moment to try to understand their limits. Sometimes, students are simply mimicking the work habits of their dedicated, hardworking parents. To those students, I usually

Chapter 4: Students—Approaching Their Uniqueness

like to give just a fair warning: watch out so you don't burn yourself out. During my years in college, I often worked and studied hard to the point where I would get a bad cold, the flu, or a minor (yet very annoying) throat infection. I always thought that was my body's warning sign, letting me know that I needed a short break. Similarly, students and parents should not ignore warning signs that might indicate that a potential breakdown (potentially worse than just a common cold) is just around the corner.

So, the most important step for students and parents alike is to try to become deeply aware of the situation as a whole. Once the student and their parents are aware that sports are affecting academics and potentially having an impact on the student's grades, that awareness will help them make the right decisions one way or another. The biggest danger is to remain in denial of the situation, ignoring that an extremely busy sports schedule may be one of the primary factors negatively contributing to a student's academic performance.

The more intense a student's sport schedule is, the more discipline is needed for the student to be able to reach a good level of balance between sports and academics. The interesting thing is that students who are very busy with sports will tend to seek more distractions to reward themselves for the efforts they

Chapter 4: Students—Approaching Their Uniqueness

invest, usually by having much more active social lives, which can often contribute to a lower level of discipline under certain circumstances. Of course, there are a great deal of dedicated sporty students with a lot of discipline, but throughout the years I have witnessed a tendency on their part to chase more "rewards" and time off. This is often no surprise, given the amount of work they put into sports while trying to perform well in academics.

So what are some other steps that can be taken by students with busy sports schedules? One often successful approach is to present the sports activities as a privilege that will be taken away unless certain conditions or requirements are met (or maintained). Personally, and especially looking from the standpoint of a student, I would suggest that such "requirements" and conditions for them to continue playing sports (at a certain level of intensity) ought to be presented as a suggestion and not as an imposition. Ideally, it should be something that the student commits to and even shares with the academic team and friends, so that the likelihood of sticking to the commitment increases (as outlined as one of our general strategies in this book).

So, what should these "requirements" or conditions be? Let's say a student plays on three different sports teams. An example of a requirement would be that he or she does an hour and a half of homework five times a week directly after sports practice in order to stay on all three teams. If this requirement isn't met, the student needs to quit one of the teams.

It is worthwhile to mention that, sometimes, leaving a specific activity simply isn't an option. In such cases, students will need to build their discipline and time management skills to succeed both at sports and academics. Naturally, one of the academic team's main goals should be to support the student in developing these skills.

Successfully Balancing Academics with Other Activities

Of course, many students also have extremely busy schedules due to activities other than sports. These could include music, work, social and other extra-curricular activities that fill up their schedules, often not leaving a lot of time for students to study hard.

Naturally, all that we have discussed above for students to balance sports and academics is perfectly applicable to students who are also very busy with other activities. It is important for them to develop their time management skills and discipline that will help them juggle all the different things they need to do to succeed in their different ventures.

What about free time? Students also deserve and need a little bit of time off to relax and recover from the craziness of their super busy schedules. As we mentioned before, students can burn out as well, so it's important for them to become aware of their boundaries and be able to respect them accordingly.

CHAPTER 5: STUDENT PSYCHOLOGY—STRATEGIES AND CONSIDERATIONS

Chapter 5: Student Psychology—Strategies and Considerations

General Strategy—Getting Students to Stick to Commitments

The strategy we are about to present and discuss certainly isn't new. It was probably invented and employed a long time ago, and it is certainly one of the most effective ways to get anyone to stick to a certain commitment. In fact, it is very likely that you have already implemented it at some point in your life in one way or another. That being said, it seems like not a lot of parents use this strategy with their children, especially when it comes to academic commitments.

So, without further ado... The strategy is simple: Get students to stick to a commitment by having them share it with other people (especially individuals who the student is closely connected to). The potential shame of not following through with the commitment usually prompts the student to embrace it fully. After all, what would everyone think? No one wants to build the reputation of a quitter. Of course, one of the biggest challenges is to get the student to go ahead and get on board with the idea of sharing the commitment with others.

One important none: It is not enough for students to share the commitments only with their

Chapter 5: Student Psychology—Strategies and Considerations

parents. That's because parents already play the role of "enforcer" often, so when they nag the student for not following through with an important commitment, the relationship between parent and child can be negatively affected. It is necessary that students share the commitment with close friends, members of the academic team, or other people they are closely connected to (in addition to their parents).

Now, how do you get the student on board with the plan? One suggestion would be for a parent to also make a commitment and share it with the student and his or her friends. Preferably, they should make a commitment that is easy to measure (and "clear cut"), like saving a certain amount of money, doing a specific number of hours of exercise per week, or anything along those lines—as long as it is somewhat challenging (especially in the eyes of the student). Of course, this strategy shouldn't be overused; it should be employed only for commitments that may have a significantly positive impact on the student's academic life.

Additionally, one should only use this strategy to get the students on board with realistic commitments. Otherwise, in case the commitment is too unrealistic, it will probably simply stress the student. If you aren't sure what is realistic, it is better to start with a small commitment first, then make it bigger later, instead of the other way around.

Getting Students to Stop Doubting Their Abilities

In today's intense and extremely competitive academic environment, it is easy for students to get discouraged and start doubting their abilities.

Too frequently, students accept the fact that they are not great at specific subjects when they can actually improve substantially through practice combined with good determination, especially when embracing the strategies we suggest in this book. The greatest problem arises when students feel hopeless, which leads to complete complacency.

In order to avoid that, it's important to contribute to the student's confidence in different ways. So here are some popular strategies to help students stop doubting their abilities:

1st – Express your belief in their skills and potential. Of course this almost goes without saying. Also, ask teachers and other respected professionals to do the same. Students deserve to hear things such as, "I know you have great

Chapter 5: Student Psychology—Strategies and Considerations

potential" or "I know you are actually (or can become) great at (fill in the blank)." Some students need to hear it more often than others. Just bear in mind, as you probably already are well aware of, that students expect parents to be inclined to say such things, so they may end up falling onto deaf ears. Extra-skeptical students will need to hear it from someone other than their parents.

2nd – Debunk myths regarding quick success and sheer "talent." It's not enough to just let them know and remind them that hard work pays off. Students must be completely convinced that skill and talent come only through hard work. For instance, let's say a student has a friend who is great at math and the student believes that this person has some sort of special magical talent that enables him to do amazing in math without major effort. Even if this person does indeed need to put much less effort than the average student into math in order to perform better, at some point in the past, he has certainly worked more than his peers. So the myth of the "naturally gifted" needs to be strongly attacked and put into question. Once the effort does lead to talent and success, they become more committed to putting more effort into academics. The common scepticism that students have regarding this theory

Chapter 5: Student Psychology—Strategies and Considerations

(that talent is primarily a fruit of consistent effort) needs to be completely destroyed.

3rd – Draw parallels between the student's success and his or her areas of struggle. For example, Anna is a successful piano player who struggles with chemistry at school. Unbeknownst to her, her confidence in music, along with the work ethic she has developed through the years in mastering piano, could assist her in achieving a good level of success in chemistry. It is easy for her to forget the struggles she had when she was still a beginner as a piano player several years ago. It is also hard for her to remember how she overcame the challenges through hard work and determination, and how those elements made her an impressive piano player. It is even harder for her to imagine that the exact same strategies could be used to enable her to succeed in virtually any school subject. Her parents and the academic team could bring this to her attention. Not only that, but constant reminders thereof could certainly benefit her tremendously and enable her to turn things around in chemistry. Of course this is a simple example but many students find themselves in a similar situation, and the areas in which they have already succeeded can bring them confidence in academic areas of struggle. Of course,

Chapter 5: Student Psychology—Strategies and Considerations

this idea is often met with scepticism. After all, what if Anna is indeed simply talented at piano and just not gifted in chemistry? For a moment, I will leave the question of interest aside; after all, she could simply argue that she just hates chemistry and loves music. But I bet she would start enjoying chemistry once some level of improvement has been achieved. Considering the question of hard work and practice, after several years of dedication to piano, Anna became a master thereof. With that in mind, if she were to take the same steps for skill improvement that she did to master the instrument and applied them to chemistry, chances are she would be able to improve significantly—as long as she maintains a level of consistent effort and dedication.

4th – Manage the expectations of the student. This is critical, because if one simply succeeds in motivating the student and boosting his or her ego (while not also pushing for persistence and hard work), unrealistic expectations can develop. It is crucial that students understand that only consistent hard work will pay off in the long run, instead of expecting success after a small period of exerting good effort. However, I can easily imagine that many students would roll their eyes when being told this idea. One good way to try to avoid this would be through sharing personal experiences of overconfidence. Who hasn't been a victim of that in the past? After hearing such stories, the student will often realize (and better understand) the dangers of overconfidence in combination with unrealistic expectations, hopefully without having to learn through experience.

Selling and Embracing Persistence

Needless to say, persistence is key in academics. Usually, students who are highly determined will be more successful than students who aren't. Therefore, parents and professionals ought to be passionate advocates of persistence and determination as they support students. With that in mind, here are some tips for helping students embrace persistence:

1st – Bring up examples from history. History is peppered with examples of impressive people who achieved success through persistence and hard work. Such examples can inspire students and lead them to change their attitude when used appropriately. Many great world leaders, for instance, have been true examples of persistence and determination. Also, most (if not all) sports legends have been fantastic examples thereof. Stories about whoever students may identify themselves with (and feel inspired by) could have a great impact on their determination, persistence, and work ethic.

2nd – Value, praise, and reward consistent effort above all else. Students need to be consistently encouraged to put consistent effort into academics, and this effort needs to be recognized. When it is, chances are the students will make it a habit of putting more and more effort into school. It is extremely important to recognize effort, even when the outcome isn't good. If a student puts a lot of effort into preparing for an exam and gets a bad grade, the effort should still be praised and perhaps even rewarded. The student also needs to be reminded that only consistent, constant effort will lead to success in the long run, and not just random outbursts of effort here and there.

3rd – Challenge the student. In many different circumstances, telling students that you know they can reach excellence as long as they have persistence can have a tremendously positive impact on their attitude. However, it is worth noting that different people respond differently to being challenged. Also, conditions might dictate the appropriate occasion in which to do it; if the student is feeling down, a challenge may simply annoy them or make them feel bad. But, as we mentioned before, imagine having someone the student truly admires telling him or her, "I truly believe you can achieve excellence in whatever you do, as long as you persist and cultivate the determination you already have within you. I challenge you to seek that within yourself and aim for nothing but excellence." Such a challenge, if done at an appropriate occasion, could have an everlasting positive impact on the student's attitude.

4th – Be careful with nagging. If a student is feeling rebellious, nagging will just be counter-productive. Also, build an awareness of the things you do and say to the student, avoiding knee-jerk reactions as soon as the potentially negative observations pop into your mind. Nagging often only leads to defiance, which is counterproductive.

5th – Don't be too soft either. Some parents (as well as educators) are a bit too flexible and soft with students. The signals are everywhere in the students' behavior—ranging to sheer defiance to an over-intolerance towards reasonable requests. When that is the case, it is important for someone to be strict enough with the student and assist him or her in becoming more disciplined. In cases like this, the role of discipline coach is very important. In extreme cases, more specialized professionals may be required.

6th – Be an example. Needless to say, just being an example of persistence and determination can have a significant impact on your child's attitude. It is, however, preferable that you don't point that out yourself too often (for obvious reasons). Leading by example can certainly be very powerful in this regard.

Debunking the "Hollywood" View of Success Once and for All

Popular films too often romanticize everything about success in an excessively unrealistic way. Too many movie characters achieve success, glory and glamour overnight and apparently without much effort. How often in fiction have we seen a story in which a talented underdog comes out of nowhere and thrives against all odds—seemingly without doing much work?

Although most students aren't consciously naive enough to actually believe such balderdash, they might subconsciously associate glamour and glory with sheer talent and not enough work. Needless to say, the absurdity and incorrectness of such an association needs to be stressed frequently. Optimally, this association should be ridiculed often. The academic team should frequently cite examples of success through hard work in order to strengthen the psychological association between persistence and success.

Handling Competition in a Healthy Way

The academic world has never been as competitive as it is today, and the intensity of competition is certainly not likely to ease off anytime soon. Therefore, it is crucial for students to handle competition with confidence and in a healthy way.

Even for very assertive students, an overly aggressive mindset towards competition can take a psychological toll that may be detrimental in academics. What do I mean by an overly aggressive mindset? A frame of mind that has a lot of negativity when thinking of competition, which would likely trigger wishes for their competitors to fail horribly. Such a mindset just simply drains one's energy, even for those who think they feed off aggressive competitiveness.

Students are substantially better off embracing a posture and a mindset of respect towards competition, the same way world class athletes do. In their quest for excellence, top competitors have the quiet confidence of those who know that true competition is within themselves only. Through embracing this healthy way of facing competition, students can become significantly more confident, while their psychological burden is diminished.

As an exaggerated illustration of such a mindset, I ask students to imagine medieval knights ready for battle. In embracing the risks associated with engaging in combat, they are confident in their carefully refined skills. They show no hatred towards their opponents; instead, they show only respect, since they all know what it takes to be a warrior. Although that might sound a bit cliché, it illustrates a healthy yet powerful competitive mindset.

Dealing with Boredom and Lack of Patience in Students

In today's society, everyone is fighting for the consumer's attention. We are all bombarded with short commercials constantly begging us to buy a product or accept an idea. This leads to our youth developing an unnaturally brief attention span, due to the psychological effect of the short bits of information being displayed everywhere, building the expectation that (subconsciously speaking) all

Chapter 5: Student Psychology—Strategies and Considerations

information ought to be as condensed and alluring as possible.

Once students' attention spans shorten as a result of this phenomenon, it becomes increasingly harder and more boring for them to sit down and focus on specific projects for long periods of time. As a result, many students complain of sheer boredom when trying to study, and their level of patience when performing complex tasks dips to extremely low levels. So how can parents and educators help change the negative impact that today's media has on young people's attention spans?

Parents and educators alike can help students develop the patience and endurance to perform complex tasks and not jump from one thing to the next before completion. Here are some strategies that may aid in the process:

1st – Challenge students with somewhat complex non-academic tasks as frequently as possible. For example, a parent could grant the student a concession (whatever that might be—a later curfew, permission to go on a trip, have friends over, etc.) in exchange for having him or her assemble a whole piece of furniture on their own, preferably a piece of furniture that isn't that easy to assemble. Or a parent could ask the student to figure out how to make a clock's hands go counter-clockwise. It can be challenging, but anyone could learn it after watching a few online videos—and it does require a bit of time and patience. These two examples might be a bit unusual, but they serve to illustrate the main idea, which is to bring students out of their comfort zone and have them exercise their patience and develop tolerance in performing complex tasks.

2nd – Help them experiment with and also establish a balance between hard work and distractions (rewards). Of course, this is nothing new to any parent. Certainly, most parents have already discussed this balance with their children hundreds of times and have also tried various strategies and experiments to help optimize the "work output" of the student—whether that is regarding homework, cleaning their room or anything to a similar effect. However, the academic team (especially the discipline coach and the tutors) can help students find an optimal balance between hard work and play in order to maximize their productivity. That also applies to how long one should study and how long one should pause for a break. An educator can help a student determine what is optimal for him or her, since everyone is different. Can a student work hard for an hour and a half before taking a break for twenty minutes, or should the student study with intense focus for just forty minutes with a shorter break instead? And after a few hard working stretches of time with alternating breaks, how long should the student spend getting a mental "reward" (which could be spending time on the computer, watching a TV show, etc.) to relax? The truth is that most students would greatly benefit from professional help combined with good experimentation in order to find what is optimal for them.

3rd – Reward and recognize sacrifice for the sake of success in academics. So let's say Bob, a high school student, skipped a night out with friends to stay home and study hard for a big exam coming up. He gave up something fun and enjoyable for the sake of academic success. His parents should recognize and reward that accordingly, since it signals a commitment to excellence, and that should be encouraged.

CHAPTER 6: CASE STUDIES

Melanie (Busy Student & Academic Team on a Budget)

"Melanie was in her sophomore year when her intense commitment to gymnastics began to have an effect on her school grades. Cutting down on her training hours wasn't an option, so her mother had to find a way to help her thrive in both gymnastics and school while on a budget. With much determination, Melanie's mother was able to provide her with enough support throughout the remaining years of high school to overcome the time constraints, make the best of her time, and thrive—leading her to gain acceptance to her program of choice at a renowned college under a gymnastics scholarship."

Melanie had already been doing gymnastics for several years when she started getting low grades in her sophomore year of high school. Before that, she was able to do well in school, despite her intense commitment to gymnastics. The problem seemed to be that the subjects were getting a lot harder in her sophomore year, so the limited time she had to dedicate to her studies no longer seemed to be enough. After a few intense discussions with her mother, it was evident that gymnastics was a true and deep passion of Melanie's, so quitting was simply not an option. Although Melanie was very disciplined for a student her age, she still needed time management skills to succeed, along with enough academic support in order to overcome the recent road bumps that she started to hit.

Melanie's mother, Tess, was willing to do whatever she could to help. However, she was on a tight budget, which seemed to give her limited options for putting an academic team together, since she wouldn't be able to afford the help of expensive professionals. Melanie needed help in math, science, and English. Additionally, she initially needed some motivation in order to keep her head high so she could overcome the hit that the lower grades had on her confidence. So Tess started to look for help in a variety of different places—from her personal connections to local college bulletin boards.

Through Melanie's gymnastics coach, Tess was able to find a retired math teacher, Jeremy, who was willing to tutor Melanie for an affordable price. Additionally, Tess found a college student in her junior year, Debbie, who could tutor both English and science for a small fee. Debbie had a great personality and had success as a dancer and as a cheerleader, while she still did quite well in academics. Melanie developed a great relationship with Debbie, who was able to motivate and inspire her while providing her with academic support. Debbie was able to help Melanie for two years until her own college graduation, since she then planned to start a job in a different city. By that time, Melanie only needed support with English and she no longer needed help with science. Although it was somewhat sad for Melanie to stop working with Debbie, who had been a great mentor, she learned a lot of good strategies to succeed in academics while juggling different activities.

During Melanie's sophomore year, Tess was able to find an excellent consultant that could help Melanie make the right choices to get into her college program of choice. The consultant's cost was a bit high but was still affordable, since they would only need to meet few times. Given that Melanie had a somewhat clear idea of what she wanted to pursue in college, the consultant was able to point her in the right direction with course selection and potential choices for colleges, especially including those that would actually offer highly competitive gymnastics scholarships.

Unfortunately, around the time that Debbie had to move away and could no longer help Melanie, Jeremy started to have some health issues and let Tess and Melanie know that he would need some time off from tutoring math. The timing was a bit rough—this was right before Melanie's final exams in her junior year of high school—so she needed to work really hard and find as much support as she could get within her means in that time period. Fortunately for her, she had already developed enough confidence in the most important subjects. For math, Melanie was able to find a tutor that worked with a friend of hers, and they would get tutoring together for an hour and a half every week in order to share the costs. Although that wasn't necessarily optimal, the tutoring sessions went well enough for Melanie to prepare for her exams. Additionally, Melanie was actively watching instructional math videos online that helped her grasp the concepts she was struggling with.

Melanie's senior year of high school was a bit of a marathon as she juggled her gymnastics with academics in order to maintain a respectable GPA. In the end, she was able to obtain an impressive scholarship at a renowned college for her program of choice. However, her success may have not been possible if she hadn't stepped it up in her sophomore year with the assistance of Debbie and Jeremy. Naturally, Tess' determination to help her daughter also made a tremendous difference, along with the investments she had to make in the process.

Duncan (Independent Student with a Low B Average)

"Duncan was a student getting a low B average going into his sophomore year of high school. An independent student, Duncan usually made decisions together with his parents where his academics were concerned. With the help of a math tutor and later an English tutor who also acted as a discipline coach, Duncan progressively increased his grades in high school, with his sights set on attending business school. Despite occasional struggles, Duncan succeeded in achieving his college program of choice."

Duncan was in his sophomore high school year when he started working with Jake, a math tutor. Duncan was a B student in math but had struggled the previous year with a teacher he had found to be challenging at school. Duncan and his mother decided that he would take math in eleventh grade through a distance education program along with hiring a tutor, so they hired Jake, a local tutor with an independent tutoring business. They set up two weekly sessions of an hour and a half each in order to go over the content, while relying on Duncan to

Chapter 6: Case Studies

work on his own for a few hours a week in order to practice and advance throughout the course. Additionally, Jake would usually chat with Duncan's parents about twice a month with updates on his progress.

As they worked together, Duncan and Jake started to build rapport, and the results started to show that the system they had in place was definitely working. Duncan's confidence in math was rising and that confidence began to translate into other subjects at school. Compared to the previous year, Duncan's level of stress was much lower, since he was no longer struggling with math. This enabled him to focus more of his time on different subjects.

However, it wasn't all going perfectly for Duncan. It became clear that Duncan had developed some habits that were detrimental for him as a student. His organizational skills were terrible, and he would often forget about assignments and exam dates rather frequently. Something needed to be done in order to get him to overcome these detrimental habits and to develop skills that would later be of great benefit to him in college.

Jake gained the respect and the trust of Duncan's family, and they entrusted him to try to help Duncan regarding his organizational skills.

Considering the four essential roles of an ideal academic team, Duncan already seemed to have the necessary support of the technical instructor (since he wasn't feeling challenged by any other subject other than math). Since he was highly motivated himself, finding a motivator was not a priority. However, Duncan was missing a planner and a discipline coach. A planner would assist him in having more direction in his academics. He was the kind of independent student that would benefit from more specific goals, since he wasn't entirely sure what the post-secondary programs that interested him actually required. Having more specific goals would give him a stronger sense of purpose and direction. Additionally, a good discipline coach would help him to get organized and focused.

Jake and Duncan's parents knew of a local educational consultant that could assist him in developing a rough plan for getting into his post-secondary institutions of choice, which was also useful in determining what courses he should primarily focus on while in high school. Given that he was interested in getting accepted into a few specific business schools, the importance of a few core courses became clear and evident—especially mathematics and English.

Chapter 6: Case Studies

In addition to the planner that assisted Duncan, his parents decided to also hire an English tutor for Duncan—Fiona, who worked with Jake—who had a reputation for building a connection with students and assisting them in developing a good level of discipline and organization. So, in addition to working with Duncan on raising his grades in English as high as possible and continuously improving his writing skills with college in mind, she would push him to develop the skills that he lacked in terms of organization, preparation, and self-control. Given that Duncan was a very independent student with an active social life, she knew that instilling discipline into his work habits could potentially be a tall task, despite the fact that he had signalled that he was on board with the idea. Duncan and Fiona settled on one hour and a half session every week to get started. About every month, they would re-evaluate and decide whether or not to change the frequency of the sessions.

Fiona and Duncan's parents agreed that it would be a good idea for her to initially build rapport with Duncan while tutoring him in English before trying to focus on his discipline. Then, once a connection was established and Duncan developed a good deal of admiration and respect for Fiona, she could start tackling more of the issues that needed attention.

Despite his busy soccer schedule, Duncan was able to juggle the English and math tutoring sessions on a regular basis. Initially, Duncan was somewhat shy working with Fiona. However, after a few weeks of English tutoring, Duncan started to progressively become more open with her. Fiona then started to chat with him about what he perceived as his needs in terms of getting more organized. Since Duncan was continuously improving his grades in English, Fiona suggested that they would then get together for an hour's worth of English tutoring, followed by half an hour of discipline coaching. Given the quality of the tips and strategies that Fiona gave Duncan, he started seeing the value of the coaching, especially in view of his interests in post-secondary education.

After a few months, Jake asked Duncan how things were going with Fiona. Duncan confessed that he wouldn't have been as accepting of the tips and strategies about discipline if she weren't as personable and charismatic as she was. It was evident that the rapport that they had built was essential in their relationship.

In his junior and senior years of high school, Duncan decided to tackle math at school again, especially after building his confidence and doing well in distance education during his sophomore year. In his last years of high school, Duncan's math teacher Mr. Simmons was very easy going. However, Duncan still kept working with Jake in order to maintain his strong performance in mathematics.

During the junior year, Fiona and Duncan kept working together once a week for an hour and a half at a time, occasionally meeting more often whenever there was an important assignment in his English class or whenever an important essay was due. The commitment remained throughout his senior year, although they focused primarily on the English tutoring in order to make sure he was prepared to write well in college. Duncan did go through occasional spells in which his discipline wavered, especially when he was more intensely involved in his sports teams. However, the frequent meetings with both Fiona and Jake (especially since the two worked as a team) would frequently remind him of the importance of staying organized and disciplined.

Chapter 6: Case Studies

Christopher (From Barely Passing to Straight As)

"After an extremely poor performance in his sophomore year of high school, Christopher's parents were somewhat desperate. They were afraid that Christopher would continue to be distracted by playing video games for several hours a day during his junior year as well. However, things took a major turn during his junior year after a strict math tutor, also performing the role of a motivator, helped to boost Christopher's confidence, enabling him to turn things around. Keeping things up in his senior year, Christopher was able to get accepted into a highly reputable college, but not directly into his program of choice. Maintaining his high grades in his freshman year of college with the help of a quality academic team, Christopher was able to transfer into the business school at his college, attaining his goal."

Christopher started his junior year of high school knowing that something needed to be changed. In the previous year, his grades had been extremely low—he had barely passed several subjects. He knew that he was guilty of focusing primarily on playing video games during his sophomore year. However, he did have a few things that played in his favor. The most important one was that he had the feeling he had the overall potential to do well in school. The second most important thing, perhaps, was that he was ambitious. His parents constantly demonstrated that they believed in him. That being said, Christopher was often stubborn and defiant towards his parents.

Christopher's parents had tried other options before. A retired teacher who briefly tutored him in English had attempted to assist him with organizational skills and focus. However, he didn't respond well—there was never a connection. After her, a young biology tutor also failed to make a good impression. Instead of being helpful in making him focus, the biology tutor would frequently be bossed around by Christopher given his strong personality, so it soon became evident that not much would come out of that tutoring relationship.

Christopher's parents knew that he needed someone who would stand up to him and lead him with a strong hand to turn things around. Early in his junior year, they found Jake, a math tutor who had a reputation for motivating and inspiring his students. Once they met with Jake, they let him know of the situation and that he should be strict with Christopher if they were to succeed in working together.

Once they met, Christopher showed promise but tried to make it clear that he would call the shots and work as hard as he found necessary, nothing more. During the initial meeting, Jake realized that Christopher was actually afraid of having a poor academic performance like in the previous year. So, Jake challenged Christopher to step it up while letting him know that he would be in charge and that he would make Christopher work hard in order to succeed. Since other professionals would usually comply with all of Christopher's requests (perhaps in an attempt to make him happy and to keep him as a customer), he wasn't used to someone being strict with him. That in itself made Christopher gain respect for Jake. Interestingly enough, Jake wouldn't usually go for the strict approach. However, he found that it was the optimal approach, given Christopher's personality, as well as the surrounding circumstances.

Jake found that the discrepancy between Christopher's ambitions and his recent grades at school were bothering him. It was clear that he wanted to succeed, so Jake continuously challenged Christopher from the start, constantly offering him a taste of what reality would be like if he didn't step it up. Despite the frequent whining, Christopher actually started working harder than he had ever worked before. Jake would also frequently remind Christopher of his potential to do well in school in order to light a fire under him. After regular sessions (usually between three to four hours of math tutoring sessions a week), Christopher started experiencing a steep increase in his math grades. Meanwhile, Christopher's parents also hired a tutor that would support him in social sciences, since his grades needed a bit of a boost in that area as well.

Additionally, despite Jake's good level of strictness, Christopher's parents found the need to find him a discipline coach in order to help him develop enough self-mastery and focus to study as frequently as he needed given his goals. A family friend of Christopher's parents named Michael, a retired lieutenant, offered to become part of the academic team. His no-nonsense style was a good match for Christopher, who responded well to Michael's efforts. They would meet only twice a month for breakfast, early in the morning, to discuss Christopher's progress at school and techniques to stay focused.

Continuing with the frequent sessions and hard work, Jake and Christopher went through ups and downs, ultimately leading to a final math exam grade in his junior year of over 90%. However, that wasn't after Jake had to put up with Christopher's extensive whining throughout the process.

Throughout Christopher's senior year of high school, he was able to maintain a high grade point average across all core subjects, leading to his acceptance into his college of choice. However, he wasn't able to get directly into his program of choice. That being said, he kept his hopes alive, given that a great performance in his freshman year of college would afford him the opportunity to get into the renowned program he had originally wished for.

Christopher also continued to meet with Michael on a regular basis, continuously getting more tips and strategies on becoming more focused and disciplined. The level of respect that he developed for Michael was enough to actually lead him to do a significant amount of studying and hard work, despite whining and complaining frequently to Jake.

Jake was in charge of providing Christopher with academic support in various freshman college subjects. When he wasn't comfortable with a specific topic himself, he hired a qualified subject expert to do so on his behalf. Meanwhile, Christopher's commitment continued to increase throughout his freshman year.

After a successful freshman year, Christopher applied to his program of choice and was accepted.

Chapter 6: Case Studies

The days when he was a struggling sophomore with no discipline were left far behind.

www.ingramcontent.com/pod-product-compliance
Lightning Source LLC
Chambersburg PA
CBHW071847230426
43671CB00012B/2089